# "HANDS ON MARKETING
## FOR THE BUSY, GROWING BUSINESS"

*By*

# Colin Rees

 Published by Quest Publishing, The Courtyard, Hertford, Herts, SG14 1EQ
ISBN number: 0 9529096 4 2.

*"Small businesses are not some minority interest - they are the backbone of the British economy"*

**John Major**

## HOW VITAL IS YOUR GROWING BUSINESS TO THE BRITISH ECONOMY?

**These quotes were specially requested by the author for this book.**

*"Stakeholders in a modern economy will today, more frequently than ever before, be self-employed or small businesses. We should encourage this, diversify the range of help and advice for those wanting to start out on their own to allow them to do so successfully."*

**Tony Blair**

*"Britain's potential is enormous. The vitality, dynamism and talent of the British people are second to none. Small and medium sized enterprises are often the most innovative and dynamic in any given industrial sector. Britain needs competitive firms that make the best use of their intelligence, creativity and skills to harness competitive growth and to build a society in which opportunity is available to all and where advancement is through merit."*

**Margaret Beckett**

*"Thriving small firms are vital to the success of the economy. They are the innovators and risk takers, and therefore the creators of wealth and jobs. Small businesses make an enormous contribution to the economy and to society."*

**William Hague**

*"Free enterprise thrives on the hard work of many people running small businesses. Without them, we would all be the poorer and our own lives that much more difficult".*

**John Redwood**

*"Small businesses are the engine room of the British Economy."*

**Nick Harvey**
Liberal Democrat Trade and Industry spokesman on small businesses.

## FOREWORD

If a retail business can lose up to 30% of its customers in the course of the year, and this is the average loss for retailers, what percentage customer loss does the average company selling to other businesses experience? This statistic demonstrates the supreme importance of conducting marketing properly, but there are barriers.

In a small or medium sized business, time is at a premium and those in charge are expected to be experts in everything; a wizard accountant, a top personnel manager, a distribution specialist and it helps if there is some industry knowledge too.

Above all, the ability to recognise and capture a particular market, selling just the right range of goods at exactly the correct prices to maximise profit is a paramount skill which most general managers are not born with. It takes years of practice, an affordable budget and lots of time to think and develop. Most managers do not have that time, but the effective application of **marketing** for business development is a very strong tool in the promotional armoury of any size business, particularly one run by the owner.

Almost anyone managing a small to medium sized business will be aware of the problem. You look for new business. When it comes in, it is vital to concentrate on servicing it properly and while you do that, you have no time to sell. When the contracts in hand are complete, there is no new business and the whole process starts over again.

This phenomenon I call; *'the growing business cycle'*, and almost every small business suffers from it to varying degrees. Even established firms with specialist staff are still guilty of not seizing every possible opportunity. This is normally the result of a lack of defined management priorities, a failing in efficiency or communications, or a problem with planning and implementation.

There are two other possible reasons; *"We've always done it like that,"* and everyone's always *"just too busy."*

As our education system improves, as more people enter the commercial world with a university education, consumers as a group become more discerning. While people generally may be more prosperous, consumers are less secure in employment or personal, financial commitment. They are naturally more sceptical of claims, they have fixed opinions and in simple terms, they are less easily *'taken in'*.

I have always tried to avoid defining *'marketing'*. Everyone offers a different explanation and all will be correct to some extent. However, I have found one worthy enough to pass on.

*"Marketing - All the things you do to make the telephone ring.*
*Selling - All the things you do after you pick up the phone."*

Harvard Business School.

Any entrepreneur seeking to build a formidable sales function will avoid marketing at their peril, for however you define it, the power that stands behind the title is a greater resource to a growing business than water is to the Sahara.

The marketing discipline does not start with the business that wants to make more profit, nor with the MD who in many firms is all-powerful, but sometimes wrong. It starts with the consumer, for it is he or she who decides your commercial fate. What you **can** do is to be as certain as possible that the circumstances are correct for your customers to buy from you with ease and it is **here** that marketing skill comes into its own.

Your prospect is not another company - it is a person who works at your customer's company, an average consumer who is responsible for ordering your product or service. If you can identify your prospect consumer exactly, the task of deciding how to sell into that market becomes easier. If you have not taken the time to look at your real aims and objectives, or if the process is somewhat *'stale'*, even if you are just hoping for annual increases in profitability, then this practical book, written in *'easy-speak'* will help by defining a simple, structured, logical way forward.

The main problem is that any lack of knowledge is probably losing you profit. For example, if you run a promotion badly, you miss some response and as well as losing profit from those missed sales, you miss capturing on-going sales from those new customers. You lose quite a lot by doing it wrong.

Marketing does not need to be a complex, scientific discipline unless that is your perception. Largely it is the application of practical common sense which is impossible to consider logically, or in any detail in the heat of the working day.

*"Hands On Marketing"* has been written for busy people who know, promotionally speaking, what they should have done months ago, but still haven't done it. If you know nothing about a subject, read the section and apply it to your business circumstances. If you still cannot make these thoughts apply to your business, feel free to call me on 01992 500530. Let's see if together, we can improve your profitability.....

***Good marketing is investment, not expenditure.***
***Invested wisely, it will return over and over again.***

"HANDS ON MARKETING For the busy, smaller business"

## CONTENTS

### Chapter 1
### PLANNING AND PREPARATION
*Initial research and decisions leading to the marketing plan.*

### Chapter 2
### THE  MARKETING FUNDAMENTALS
*The things you need to think about before you carry out your plan.*

# Chapter 3 - MARKETING METHODS

*Twenty three ways to increase your sales and profitability.*

**MARKETING METHODS - CONTINUED**

**Chapter 4**
**MARKETING FACTORS FOR CONSIDERATION**
*These are subjects that will help to increase profits*

## Chapter 5
## PUTTING ALL OF IT TOGETHER
*What action to take now that you know*

## Chapter 6
## THE MARKETING FUTURE

## Chapter 7
## THE  CONCLUSION

**SPECIAL READER OFFER  PAGE 204**

## INTRODUCTION

*Where is your business placed against the national trend?*

Economic indicators are good. The UK unemployment graph has shown a gradual decline since 1993. The housing market, the central indicator of consumers' fortunes, is showing a marked rise, the first in 5 years. Inflation appears to be under control and consumer spending is showing general increases.

Retail spending by consumers has been rising gradually as we emerge from recession, and retail sales have risen by 0.03% month on month. So, at the moment, UK commerce is buoyant.

For some time now, it has been apparent that marketing in terms of small businesses in the UK requires some hard examination, particularly those businesses run by the owner, director, or main shareholder. Yet, there is no point in starting to look carefully at the way a business operates without being honest about exactly what is done and why.

If the reasons are purely historical, defended by phrases such as, *"We've always done it like that"*, then there's every reason for a very close examination indeed. An individual commercial business can easily lose a high percentage of its customers every year through natural wastage. People move away, people pass away, people are attracted away. So if each business in the UK is losing customers, where are they going?

Perhaps your business is managing to attract enough new customers to replace the ones lost and so you see little change. Equally, you see no growth. The promotional cycle should never stop. In any business, it is a constant round of increasing the numbers of people through the door and encouraging them to spend more by *'selling up'*. Research is the only way to keep track of what is happening.

Most managers are so busy, that looking carefully at the business, just for a moment, is not high on their list of priorities. I well remember one MD as he showed me around his business saying *"We only stop to sleep."* He worked from 6.00 am to 12.30 pm seven days a week, so perhaps he had an excuse. But if everyone in the country is as desperately busy as we all make out, how can it be that our country is not number one in the commercial world order, despite having the strongest economy in Europe? So is all this busy-ness getting us anywhere? Are we so busy because we are working inefficiently?

Assessing priorities from the proper footing of basic research is the route towards maximum efficiency in every job. If you are running at maximum efficiency, being effective the entire time, do you work to a prioritised job list that you completed the evening before? Do you stop after each task and re-assess? Self analysis is vital to growth and that's our starting point.

# CHAPTER 1

## PREPARATION

*The first chapter opens with the planning stage. Planning is central to maximising your promotional response and you **can** do it better with a little more knowledge. Every growing business needs to know where it is and where it is going. This is achieved by creating a marketing plan which this chapter leads you to.*

This chapter covers:

- What is the starting point when one is so busy?

- Where is your business now?

- Where do you want it to be?

- What are your goals?

- Some basic, simple, quick and easy research in the shape of a SWOT analysis.

- What is unique about your business in comparison to your competitors?

- Where do you '*position*' your brand or company in the market place?

- The marketing plan and how to prepare it.

***Working in a planned way is the secret to over-achieving, in an environment where there is no time to think.***

## HOW DOES A BUSY MD PROMOTE?

While I was writing this chapter, two faxshots landed on my desk from a company selling water coolers. I am always intrigued to see how a small company markets themselves and so I rang the local office number listed on the fax to ask why I had been faxed **two** copies. The local number was a private home. Then I called the London Head Office, asking to speak to someone in authority. *"I'll put you through to Serena,"* the voice said. I explained my annoyance at receiving two copies, the wrong telephone number, and the fact that just last week, I had ordered one of their products on a one month trial. What mistakes does this experience demonstrate?

*Mistake number 1* - Why send two faxshots when you can upset people by sending just one?
*Mistake number 2* - Wrong telephone number; someone did not check a proof *'just in case'*.
*Mistake number 3* - Using Serena's first name makes you wonder what authority she has.
*Mistake number 4* - Nobody checked the list for duplicated addresses.

That's four simple, completely unnecessary errors. So how did the MD explain them? When I reached him, his explanation was hardly credible. They were *"only a small firm,"* this was their first use of faxshots, they had used a professional agency to send a test run of 2000 faxshots, and so far that morning they had four responses of which three were complaints.

*Mistake number 5* - The agency was *'recommended by a friend,'* and they had never met.
*Mistake number 6* - Giving the reason for poor performance as being *'a small company'*.

Company size has nothing to do with planning and executing a promotion properly. As well as losing profits through reduced response, the example shows just how much goodwill can be lost.

There is no doubt this company lost profits from the exercise and even if you are not making as many classic errors as this firm did, if you are not promoting correctly, you will hardly produce the maximum response. This means, you lose profit. What a splendid example of budget wasting.

*Communication is the responsibility of the sender.*

How does a busy MD promote? Badly if it is conducted by the *'seat-of-the-pants'* method, where an immediate sales increase is required, a promotion is not planned, is poorly executed and therefore receives a diminished response.

Worse is the loss from repeat sales, over a prolonged period, those missed customers will bring you if you look after them properly.

The first letters of that method are S, T, O & P. This MD definitely wished he had never bothered, but, however busy you may be, promotions **can**, and must be mounted properly to reap the full reward from your investment.

### SUMMARY

- However *'small'* your business may be, you do not need to waste budget and lose profit by running ineffective promotions.

- The extent of your success can be directly related to the time you devote to being inventive and planning properly.

- Remember just how much you stand to lose if you promote badly.

*The most damaging attitude to a growing business is encapsulated
in the phrase; "We've always done it like that"*

## THE STARTING POINT

*Before you can begin to establish a growth programme using the marketing discipline, you need to examine your entire business and do some basic research. In essence, marketing is all about raising sales and profits by creating an appropriate sales environment.*

### WHERE IS YOUR BUSINESS PLACED NOW?

An initial review of your business might include your production process, distribution network, product specification as well as the markets currently open to you and how you have arrived at your present position. Your product sourcing, accounting procedures and computer capability are other factors you need to examine.

So **marketing** in this context is only one of the disciplines that needs close examination as a part of the whole process of establishing just exactly where you are and where you want your business to be.

### MARKET RESEARCH

Examination of the sales potential is essential:
- what *type* of person will buy from you
- what to sell
- how to '*develop*' what you sell
- can you sell to them more than once
- is there a '*pension product*' such as on-going maintenance
- how many of each might they buy
- what compliments your range
- what price would they consider good value

Finding out what potential customers think is the logical starting point before launching a new product or service.

Established businesses often lose sight of the '*worth*' of conducting market research. Speaking to prospects and customers through telephone research, face to face or by using questionnaires defines your target exactly. It crystallises the best way to reach them to maximise sales.

- **IDEA**: You need to conduct some initial research and make some decisions before you start the planning process that leads to creating a marketing plan, the eventual objective of this chapter. The best starting point is a SWOT analysis.

Providing you are totally honest, you can establish exactly where your business is, what sort of avenues may be open to you to improve profits and the areas you should look at quickly.

## THE SWOT ANALYSIS

*SWOT stands for Strengths, Weaknesses, Opportunities and Threats. A number of different SWOT analyses can be carried out.*

This exercise should be a regular part of the necessary self-assessment of the business or its integral parts and it is the way a marketing professional will assess your position to make recommendations. (See the reader offer on Page 204).

It should be conducted at least twice a year - more often if possible. You may choose to look carefully at the staff, a particular area of your business, or even yourself.

**HELP HINT**:   Research is best conducted with the help of an outsider with no past history or internal politics to cloud the result.

Taking the business first, isolate the strengths, weaknesses, opportunities and threats. Aspects such as the staff, location, premises, product range, pricing policy, all can be examined within these categories.

Here is an example carried out recently with a business in the South. This is part of what the MD of a medium-sized, engineering-related company said about his own business in answer to the question, *"What are your strengths?"*

### STRENGTHS

- *My partner is adept at product sourcing*
- *I'm pretty good at finance*
- *Customer contact is very good and we have an excellent database*
- *General systems, sales and marketing systems, accounting systems and procedures run well*
- *We are financially sophisticated*
- *Freehold property*
- *Artistic flair*
- *Hands on approach to technology, directors understand how things work*
- *Own workshops, know what's going on, close to markets and products*

So how can this Manager use his strengths to help him? The sales systems are good - does that permeate through the organisation or is this opinion held just at management level? Artistic flair is a definite strength in this company as they design test equipment. Usually, it suggests innovation, a key requirement in successful marketing. Sometimes strengths are in fact, opportunities as well.

## WEAKNESSES

- *Do not sell up*
- *Do not have face-to-face contact with big companies*
- *Do not use market information fully*
- *Reluctance to visit customers except where demonstratively worthwhile*
- *Lack of use of some systems by sales staff*
- *Need a middle management layer*
- *Do not spend enough time on strategic thought*
- *Less creative, lack of marketing spark*
- *Exhibitions are very weak indeed*

It is often this section that reveals where positive action could suggest a whole list of priorities. What can you see here? If you are totally honest in identifying your weaknesses, you will immediately see areas to address that lead to the creation of a list of '*action*' priorities. Selling up can immediately improve your profits.

## OPPORTUNITIES

- *Our biggest competitor has a huge market share but hasn't advertised much lately*
- *Explicit customer base, 5000 customers*
- *Grow sales to wholesalers, presently only 20 - 30% of the business*
- *Increase product range slowly*
- *Exports to ex-Commonwealth countries is an opportunity*
- *Salesman/Rep. We could do with one*
- *Consumer, mail order*
- *Other industrial markets*

Once again, it is clear what might be done to improve and expand the business. Listing opportunities creates its own priorities. The first job in this case should be getting into that huge customer base with a series of multiple special offer promotions designed to sell more products to new customers and different product ranges to present customers. Having no external sales person is a weakness and an opportunity.

## THREATS

- *The political situation in the Far East. We may need replacement suppliers*
- *If the biggest competitor mounts a specifically targeted campaign, especially if price aggressive*
- *Over market, over spend, a method fails - bad marketing decisions*
- *Dead customers are lost forever*
- *Bad product*

Threats are often few in number but significant in ramification. The first threat that most clients mention is competition. Competition sometimes can become an opportunity if you can establish where they are making their mistakes. Remember, a high percentage of their customers are disappearing each year as yours will if you do nothing to keep or replace them. Later in the book, there is a whole section devoted to competing.

Lapsed accounts may be retrievable which classifies them as *'opportunities'* as you can get the business back. A lost account is a *'threat'* if it has gone to your competitor. Your lack of knowledge of promotions could be a *'threat'* if they are badly executed and losing profit or a *'strength'* if you plan them well.

### *The more you know, the more you grow.*

You may consider it unnecessary to conduct a SWOT analysis as it will not tell you anything you do not know already. However, there is a difference in *'knowing'* about matters and having them on paper in an orderly fashion where they can be acted upon and the information used.

- **IDEA**: Conduct a SWOT analysis to tell you what the problems are. The strength of this exercise lies in the final prioritisation of the factors contained in each list which allows you to plan subsequent actions properly, even if the actual information is not new.

Planned and conducted regularly, a SWOT analysis will establish a foundation and a set of priorities on which to build and improve, by maximising the good factors and attending to the weak. Just as important, is the opportunity it presents to examine the market which is constantly changing in a developing commercial enterprise.

### *The appendix carries a form to help you conduct your swot analysis.*

**DO IT NOW:** Try and determine which of the following fit into which of the four categories. Are these aspects strengths, weaknesses, opportunities or threats in your company?

- Your staff
- Your product, service or product range
- Your main suppliers
- Your premises
- Your delivery vehicles
- Your computer system
- The number of customers you have

See where you have put them and decide how to transform any you have listed into the *'strength'* category. If your fleet of vans all need new tyres, *van tyres* are a weakness. If you renew the tyres, they become a strength.

## WHERE DO YOU WANT TO BE?

*When you started your business, you might have used the TEC or Business Link, or you may have gone to a bank or accountant for help in taking those first few steps. Now that you are on your own, you need to decide where your business is going and specify your aims so that you can decide how your target can best be reached.*

Looking back, you may remember being asked for a business plan, a cashflow forecast and a number of other items without which it is impossible for a professional advisor to take a reasoned view on your likelihood of success or failure.

Many small and medium sized businesses have not prepared those documents since inception because time is at a premium when running your own business.

If you have no idea where you want your business to go or which markets you want to target before you move on to others, even what you personally want out of life, how can you address the way you will achieve your ambitions or objectives?

Once, when asked this question, I recall one MD of a small business telling me that the reason he started was because he wanted a Porsche.

If that was his real aim, how was he to get his Porsche? How much net profit would he need to generate before he could allocate some of that towards his personal requirement? Once we established how much he would have to sell to earn the required amount of net profit, then the questions followed as to how those sales would come in and from which markets, what extent of promotional budget was necessary, and at what staff level? It took time to establish but, once constructed, his business plan and subsequent marketing plan led directly to his required target. Your target might be different but the way to get there is the same. Identify the best market through which to attain your objective.

- **IDEA**: If you have a business plan already, you know where you are going. If you are undertaking what is known as crisis management or running from day to day with no planned goal, spend time thinking about it, then write a business plan. Stick it on the office wall. It is the reason for you being there at all.

## DECIDE YOUR USP's

*Before you can construct a marketing plan to lead you to your identified aim, a number of decisions have to be taken. It is critical to compare your brands or services with the competition and identify where you differ.*

When you have finished the SWOT analysis and decided where your business is today and what your aims are, the next stage in the planning process is to decide how to get there. This involves constructing a marketing plan, a list of actions you will undertake to produce the additional profit you need to reach your aim. One decision you must take before this next stage is to look at the business and decide what's really good about it that makes you different. This is called establishing your U.S.P.'s.

USP stands for *"unique selling proposition"* or *"unique selling point"*. That means the proposition that you will make to your prospect customers to fulfill their need, to encourage them to buy from you rather than someone else.

If your range of goods is the same as the chap down the road, what have you got that he hasn't? Maybe your staff are cheerful. So are his - this is not unique. Maybe your prices are better - he'll put his down as soon as you do then you both lose through reduced margins - this is not innovative enough. Perhaps you have a loyalty scheme and he doesn't. You might like to think in terms of **excellence** when deciding what makes your business different from a competitor.

What is truly excellent in your business? That may well turn out to be a USP. Beware of choosing *'service'* as a USP. Service is the element most business people use as a point of difference when there is no difference at all and each of us is guilty in claiming *"we give personal service"*, so this is not unique.

**CAUTION**: Beware how your prospect or customer interprets the phrase; *'personal service'*. It is quite easy to translate that as the seller handling all transactions with the buyer with no other staff involved which is largely impractical. What is really meant is that you will keep a *'watching brief'* over the account and make it your business to know what is going on - isn't it?

A very good friend who runs a menswear shop in Australia decided his USP's long ago. Every year, he travels to Europe to attend the Cologne menswear fashion exhibition where he buys thousands of dollars worth of European clothes, takes them back to Melbourne and offers his customers a unique range unobtainable elsewhere. That is a USP as his competitors do not stock such a range.

A serviced office building here in Hertford advertises the fact that theirs is the only facility in the town providing *fully furnished* offices. That is a USP no one else in that business has yet matched.

At a recent networking lunch where I spoke on this subject, one delegate took issue with me afterwards maintaining that any business or product can only have one USP. I sited this book which has a help-line, reader offer, and self-help form templates. It is reasonable to expect one element but these three together in one academic publication is unique in itself, which enables me to claim four USP's.

It could be that the unique property of your business is your skill or personality. What factor is it that can permeate through your staff to your customers?

USP's can be temporary as well as permanent. Possibly you have a promotion running such as 5% off all orders placed within twenty-four hours. Although temporary, the discount could constitute a unique selling proposition the competition does not provide. If you have decided on a *positioning statement* you will already have decided how you are unique. So, what are your USP's?

Once decided, review them each time you conduct a SWOT analysis and as the business grows and develops, your USP's keep current and positive.

## SUMMARY

- What distinguishes you from your closest competitor?

- What can you claim for your brand or your company that your closest rival can't?

- You should make sure every prospect hears about your USP's so they are aware of the main benefit of buying from you since they cannot get that benefit elsewhere.

- Do not forget that as your business grows, your USP's will probably change. This makes it at least, an annual exercise.

*Research and product planning is the starting point towards rational, effective, marketing decisions.*

## POSITIONING

*We have nearly completed the planning process which will lead to your marketing plan. There are more decisions to take concerning how to make your customers and prospects think of you first.*

Any successful product or business has won the mind of its customer. As an example, can you finish the following product positioning phrases:

*"Beanz Meanz ...."*
How about;     *"Don't just book it, XX it"*
or even;       *"A X a day helps you work, rest and play".*
And who said:   *"Soft, strong and very long".*

There seems little doubt that were I to start with the phrase;
*"The future's bright, the future's X ...."* You would definitely be able to complete the colour.

If you can complete the blanks, the branding of that product has won your mind through a *"positioning statement"*. National advertisers have learned that it is critically important to create a brand identity that customers easily recognise, remember and act upon, at the point of sale.

> ***You must create a perceivable personality for your business***
> ***that customers can identify with.***

A positioning statement, sometimes referred to as a *'strap line'* is a statement which encapsulates what you stand for in the minds of your buyers. Therefore you must first decide **how** you want customers and prospects to think of you. You may hope to be known for providing the very best value for money in which case your statement might be :

*"XYZ business - FIRST for Value".*

You may pride yourself on the range of goods you offer and wish your customers to think of you for that in which case, your positioning statement might be *"No better choice - anywhere!"*

Perhaps the attention you pay to your customers is important to you. *"XYZ Business - If we haven't got it, we'll get it - fast!".*

A *'combined'* positioning statement can cover more than one factor such as: *"No. 1 for Quality, Value and Service".*

These examples demonstrate the point but lack ingenuity and sparkle. Ideally, a positioning statement or strapline will encapsulate your individual area of excellence, the fact that sets you apart from competitors or the central marketing direction you are taking at this time.

A good example comes from *"Cellnet, the net that sets you free"* or more *recently "the big network"*. The strapline changed as the marketing direction the company wished to implant in the mind of their customers altered to illustrate the widest coverage of cells against competitors' networks.

What do you think these businesses are trying to achieve in the following positioning statements? Texas DIY stores have adopted the phrase: *"Where more costs you less."*

*"Get wise, call the guys"*

This last positioning statement was seen on a van run by a windscreen replacement company. This is a good example of a strap line which *could* convey a negative reaction in the mind of the customer as it may imply the proverbial *'cowboy'* trades-person.

The use of such slang as *'the guys'* could irritate, as it sets a low tone and prospective customers wouldn't think they were not wise anyway. You want to be thought of favourably. If you choose the wrong phrase, you might be remembered for negative reasons. On the other hand, this company may see the phrase as one which appeals to the customer they wish to attract.

A well constructed statement can have the opposite effect. *"Our fish are so fresh, we haven't had time to inform the next of kin"*. That was on the back of a van delivering in Birmingham.

An insurance agency client developed an insurance product that was specific to a market no one else was addressing. He was a small business but managed to get support for his plan from underwriters and called me in to help launch it. One suggestion included a positioning statement around the phrase, *"Innovation in commercial insurance"*. People were intrigued by his proposition.

It is important to choose a simple statement which is not similar to that of a rival. Many people believe the service they offer is better than anyone's. The trouble is, when one runs out of comparisons with a competitor and still finds nothing much different, service is what is left and your service might not be strong enough to use for positioning. As always, a factor which is *'individual'* to your business is likely to be more memorable. If it is too long, they will not remember it. Take a tip from the experts - Beanz Meanz ?

Consider your USP's. Can you construct a positioning statement around what is unique in your business? The serviced office company which chose the fact that they were the only company in that town offering fully furnished accommodation might focus on that fact.

*XYZ offices - We make you comfortable.*
*XYZ offices - At home today, at work tomorrow.*
*XYZ offices - We think we've thought of everything.*

Each phrase has a slightly different *'edge'* to it and conveys other factors while still partly possessing the interpretation of the furnished element. *"We make you comfortable"* suggests reliability and forethought on behalf of the customer, as well as furniture provided.

*"At home today? At work tomorrow"* reflects how easy it would be to take an office and be working the next day in a commercial environment with other business people, rather than being on your own where some find motivation difficult. The furnished USP is not conveyed directly in this statement although there could be an association with the comfort of your home.

*"We think we've thought of everything"* would only convey the furnished USP after you have agreed to look round the offices and while it is excellent in suggesting that the overall activity of this business is good, it does not address the USP directly.

These examples show that it takes considerable thought to arrive at a phrase that has the right effect in a few words, but once you have decided where you wish to position the business and you have invented your strapline, stick with it.

### *Repetition sells, repetition sells, repetition sells.......*

Do not change it, use it everywhere, internally and externally. Remember, it is intended to ensure that when your customers *think your product*, they *think you*. This association can bring much business and winning consumer minds is very much a part of the strategic battle. Can you remember who said *"Nobody does it better"?* If you cannot it must be assumed it is not used now or it has changed. This is not sensible with such a good strapline.

Older readers may remember a television brand positioning statement from a brand which has long since disappeared. *"You're never alone with a Strand"*. That must be well over 40 years ago and an example of how long such phrases can stay in the mind of a customer.

### SUMMARY

- Positioning your brand, service or company is important if you are to gain an advantage and attract prospect customers from competitive suppliers.

- If you can encourage customers to think of you first when they have a need, you are ahead of the game.

## THE MARKETING PLAN

*If you do **not** have a marketing plan together with a business plan hanging on your wall, how do you have any idea what you are doing, whether your promotions are working and whether they are worth repeating?*

Once you have made your initial decisions, you know where you are, where you want to be, and now, you have a business plan. The next logical step is to create a marketing plan to enable you to get there. In Chapter three you will find twenty three marketing methods you might use to expand your business and increase your profits.

Present research is very clear in telling us that as a working population, we are working longer and harder than when things were easy in the 80's. Although time is always at a premium, it is essential to construct a marketing plan. What time do you have in the ordinary way to take a measured view of how to maximise results from your promotional budget? How important is it to know what you will be promoting in six or twelve months time? Planning ahead keeps a market leader at the front forcing competitors to follow.

In all business enterprises, formulating a plan is the way to avoid that last minute, panic decision before a deadline. It is another reason to employ an advisor to decide, and help you execute planned promotions and surveys, to monitor all results and adjust activity to suit the changing situation. If additional sales are required, the necessary time **has to be found** to plan, implement and monitor while still performing other daily tasks.

Part of a marketing plan includes how the response will be handled efficiently. Up to 20% of all sales leads generated by a company are not acted upon. Being sharp at the front end is not a lot of help if you do not follow through.

The best way to begin constructing a plan is to list all the promotional campaigns you have undertaken this year. Start with Christmas or another high seasonal sales time and work from there. Add two extra columns and in the second, list your promotional intentions for the next twelve months.

Even a commercial company can have a January sale particularly as everyone else does at that time. What happens in Spring, how do you keep interest going in the Summer time, and what do you do to offset August and December? Estimate costs for each. Look for the gaps where there is no activity. What could you promote then? Can you think of promotions which competitors might not be mounting when you are?

Side by side with this list should run the activities you hope to undertake, such as building a database or preparing a newsletter. Add these to the plan in the third column, and cost them out.

You can inject any degree of complexity you wish, including descriptions of promotions, sales figures, ideas for new products, how to sell them and much more. A growing business will benefit more from a simple basic plan in the first year which is further developed as you gain experience.

When the Marketing plan is complete, look at the cashflow situation each month to see what the business could afford for each activity. Scale up or down according to last years' income indicators.

As the plan proceeds, enter the response, the actual cost and the estimated gross profit obtained into the last column you created. This gives vital information for next year. Compare your actual sales and profits against last year to see if your promotion had an effect in increasing on last year's figures.

As each month passes, write the plan for the same month, twelve months hence. Using the experience you gain, your promotions stay planned twelve months ahead.

*(There is a self help form in the appendix to help you to formulate a marketing plan.)*

How much more efficient will your business become by planning your activity twelve months ahead? The chances are high that if you do so, you will have an advantage over your competitors who may be working in an unplanned way as you once did.

**DO IT NOW**: Construct a basic marketing plan using these notes and the appendix form in the back. It is not difficult and at least you will be starting to think strategically about your business in a way more likely to see a return from your marketing.

SUMMARY

• The art of promoting is to decide on a plan and follow it, testing all the time, monitoring and changing it to suit the circumstances.

• What promotions have you planned to attract more customers next April? A plan on your wall will tell you.

• Are you dealing properly with every single sales lead that comes in?

• Do you have a system to tell you where all sales leads come from?

• Start a file to list the detail of each test, its yield, and what you will do next time to refine it.

# CHAPTER 2

## THE MARKETING FUNDAMENTALS

*At this stage, the basic planning should be complete, you have decided on your USP's and positioning, and you should also have a basic marketing plan on your wall.*

Before you look at the twenty three marketing methods detailed in Chapter three that you can apply to your business to take it forward, there are a few more fundamental elements to consider and decisions to take. These are important decisions, before allocating budget to marketing, as they represent your policy.

First, we look at your attitude to customers - the most vital element of the business. Service - how does yours' rate? We all claim to give superlative service. Is that claim truly justifiable? What level of budget do you need to employ on promoting, do you have a monitoring system in place, could you benefit from a customer loyalty scheme, these questions are answered.

Many companies have no idea how helpful manufacturers can be, we examine this. Innovation makes you stand out against competitors. Selling up and price perception are very important to maximising profits as is getting the most from suppliers.

Most important to any growing business is their attitude to big competitors, this chapter will help reassure you.

## CUSTOMERS ARE YOUR LIFEBLOOD

*Anyone in business knows all there is to know about customers. To start with, they're human. That means they all think differently about the same things, they all want to feel 'special' and they are all right, all of the time. Often, they do not tell you when you have upset them. Suddenly, they become part of the annual loss because something went wrong. Understanding and accepting this basic psychology, helps to keep them from suddenly disappearing.*

It is natural for everyone to think they are always right. In commerce, customers **are** always right - **always**. US advertising guru, Dave Gifford puts it this way,

> ***"The first rule in retailing is the customer is always right.***
> ***The second rule is, re-read rule one."***

GETTING TO KNOW EVERYTHING ABOUT YOUR PRESENT CUSTOMERS IS THE SINGLE MOST IMPORTANT STEP YOU CAN TAKE TOWARDS FINDING NEW ONES.

You must understand your customers completely, study the people who buy from you, predict their reactions, win their affection, know exactly how they will react to promotions and maximise their potential to you.

At a recent consultation with a new client, I asked how much was known about his present customers? *"Oh"* says the MD., *"We've got about 5000 of them here on the PC."* Indicating an excellent start, I went on to ask what sort of categories they were in, expecting SIC codes or similar.

*"Well, we put them on every day"*. In fact, they were not held in any order at all other than by the date they placed an order. That company has an impossible task getting to the core of where their business is coming from. If you know where your customers come from, it follows you know where to go to get more. This allows more direct targeting and protects against excessive promotional expenditure.

Having no defined target is a waste of promotional budget. This is sometimes referred to as a *"shotgun approach"* scattering large numbers of sales messages, but to an undefined target area. The information, in the example above was available but not in a useable form.

Using a database programme or hard copy, to remedy the situation, this client should print out the database and research every customer, re-coding into groups, starting with industry type. Marking those who have purchased within the last three months, it would be preferable to indicate which of the product group was purchased. A clear picture will emerge indicating the most successful industries.

The client can now attack those industries directly, seeking new customers in a more targeted way when before, there was considerable wastage. These actions will increase sales levels, and cost just time.

In the survey, by including the product group each customer purchased, there will be an indication of other goods they might buy, giving an opportunity to sell up to them with a different product. This is potentially the fastest source of income for him, together with recovering sales from any lapsed customers. Better targeting will save cost. He will not need more budget to achieve a more successful result and overall, his net profit will increase.

Management throughout any organisation needs to be committed to customer care and understanding. You must know the reasons why customers leave you, and the average patterns of purchasing, to be able to supply goods and services they need at the right time and price to satisfy their needs.

Many customers I have worked with over the years have had unexpected ways of reacting. Customers are individuals and you have to compensate for those differences by modifying your reaction.

In a recent survey by McGraw Hill, published by Royal Mail, it was reported that 67% of customers who take their business elsewhere do so because nobody has kept in touch with them. Constant communication is vital to customer retention. If you do nothing to keep the customers you have, if they think they have '*reduced in importance*', you will spend extra promotional budget replacing them.

Even if the number of customers is high, as with our example, it is not difficult to telephone the largest ones and write to them all, frequently. This is an excellent use for newsletters which I cover in chapter three. Even press releases and more general special offer mailings as well as telephone calls all serve to keep contact going. I heard of an executive who traveled extensively sitting at airports writing postcards just to say that he was thinking about his client's problems and would be in contact soon. Maintaining full communication with customers is critical, even when you are not fulfilling their orders, and represents another area to add to the marketing plan.

It is widely quoted that an average of 20% of customers produce 80% of your business. With five thousand customers, 20% represents one thousand customers which in turn, equates to forty calls a week or four calls per working day.

## CUSTOMER SURVEYS

The more you know about **why** people buy from you, the more you understand the need you are fulfilling and the way to attract more customers in all your promotions. Surveys and questionnaires are important in finding out and the appendix gives a sample form for you to add your questions and start using them right away.

Do you know all about your customers or do you just think you know? Where are they coming from, who are they, what industries are they in, what do they buy, where else do they go for your products, what do they truly think of you, your service and type of products?

Research is the only way to answer these questions and businesses who have tried it have something meaningful on which to base decisions. Ideally, research should be conducted regularly, at various times of the year and with a large enough sample to provide accuracy - at least 50 - 100 sets of answers.

Questionnaires are a simple, accurate way to ensure your business is running the way you think it should be. You can ask present customers whether there are other products they would like you to supply. Are your delivery times convenient, or do they have any general suggestions that could help you improve your service?

Other assessment documents are available from trade associations and various other commercial bodies. Your local Business Link can provide you with business information fact sheets on conducting market research and designing a questionnaire. Some questionnaires are very comprehensive and will give you and your advisor a planned approach to a proper, regular examination of current customer opinions.

**HELP HINT**:   A short, sample form appears at the back of this book as an appendix. Look at the information and add any questions pertaining to your business. Give each customer a small gift for completing it, for instance a pen with your name and telephone number on it. Add their name and address to your database for future mailings as they are very recent customers and assess the results. You may well be surprised at some of the answers.

Questionnaires are a critical part of the research process and they provide sales people with another reason for dialogue which in turn, may lead to an appointment or even a sale.

SUMMARY

•        Employees need to be conditioned to a customer care culture. You cannot do it alone.

•        The more you know about your customers, the more you can sell to them.

•        Does everyone in your organisation realise you are all working for the same reason, the good of the business?

•        Keep in touch with all your customers - they expect it. Conduct a survey and establish the facts.

## SERVICE

*One area where many businesses experience difficulty is service. Where products and prices are similar to those of a competitor, they rely on service as an advantage and want the copywriter to focus on service as the only reason why a prospect should try them. But how justified is it, within your firm, to claim that your service is 'second to none'?*

In Britain today, in industrial and commercial circles, we seem to have a relaxed attitude to customer service. We all like to *think* our company provides optimum service and if you wish to retain your customers, optimum service is precisely what you must provide. Some companies are very successful at training staff to live by the pretext that **'the customer is king'**. Those who do so will always have an advantage over those who do not.

*"Service"* is the single greatest area in which a company can show a real difference from a competitor. Good service is so simple to achieve but **very** difficult to execute on a continuing basis unless it becomes ingrained in the company culture, producing automatic reflexes from dedicated staff.

If service really is good in your company, say so in the corporate brochure, spell out exactly the areas in which you excel, which is what potential customers want to hear.

Poor service is one of the most damaging factors to a customers' perception of your business, and can easily lead to the loss of an account. Think of the effort that went into gaining it, the hurdles you overcame to keep it running smoothly: surely it is worth fighting to keep?

- **IDEA**: One way to show customers that you have thought about ways to improve your overall service levels is to establish a defined disputes procedure in case something does go wrong. Does your company have a disputes policy? If it does, certain people will be following a pattern of damage limitation effectively, to end a bad situation with an intact and satisfied customer.

Like everything else, a complaint dealt with immediately when everyone is so busy may not be handled in the best way. A complaints procedure is a necessary starting point in ensuring your survival. Things can and do go wrong, now and then, for none of us is infallible.

By *'service'* do you mean getting it right every time, always being pleasant and cheerful to customers, whatever your feelings? Why not establish a general attitude throughout your company of pride in the job and a good end result; happy customers who come back? Two of my clients have set up offices on the premises of their biggest customers in order to look after their accounts properly and quickly - that's good service. Have you ever been in a sandwich bar where they offer to cut the crusts off? If you don't like crusts, that's good service.

Service means *'going that extra mile'* for the customer. It is an area requiring very close examination in most companies. In dispute situations with customers, it is not a matter of who is right or wrong, they are **always** right. Where good service is concerned, you are never able to have *'off'* days. You go to work to look after customers and fully satisfy their buying needs, nothing else matters. That means considerable sacrifices from your staff and constant reminders that the customer is the most important item on the commercial agenda.

- **IDEA**: Why not open half an hour early on your slowest day next week, put a sign on the front door and a message on the answerphone saying *'closed for staff training'?* Sit down with your staff and talk about customer service. Make it the first of many discussions and use it to motivate them, tell them of your objectives, tell them you want to substantiate a reputation for using a phrase such as, *"nobody serves you better."*

You need to create a culture where all staff understand that providing the best possible customer service is now the ethos. Watch over the next few weeks and see how good results can flow from involving the people who serve your customers and take your money for you.

### *Good service means paying supreme attention to detail- however you feel*

Recently, I took space in a trade directory for a year on a test basis. I asked for a voucher copy to ensure the entry had been made and when the item was published, the voucher copy duly arrived. While a book mark had been provided, it was not placed at the page where my advertisement appeared and it took me 15 minutes to find our entry.

The invoice had been received two weeks earlier, before I even saw the voucher copy. Is that a company who demonstrates a true concern for customer care? If questioned, I am perfectly certain they would tell me of their *"personal service"*, as most companies honestly believe they provide. They didn't upset me but nor did they go *'the extra mile'*.

If you realise that you cannot complete a job by the time you promised your customer, tell them. There is nothing worse than expecting something from a supplier that does not arrive when expected and it is one of the fastest ways to loose goodwill. Being completely honest is the quickest way to secure a customer.

**YOUR SWITCHBOARD COULD BE THE FASTEST ROUTE TO A POOR IMPRESSION.**

Consider what happens when a new caller telephones your company for the first time. There is nothing more infuriating than telephoning for information at 9.00 am to be greeted with the answering machine or just the ringing tone, especially when the caller started work at 8.00 am.

How do you greet your customers? The person who answers your phone gives that first, vital impression to a new caller.

*"Hello, XYZ builders merchants, Mandy speaking, how can I help you".*

This is a very common first response designed to be ultra helpful and to sound efficient. Unfortunately, it takes vital seconds before the caller is given the opportunity to state their reason for calling and *'How can I help you'* really is not *'different'* any more. Frankly, a busy manager will find this highly annoying, your company sounds like a soundbite, and most buyers are people with very little time to waste.

Shrink your company name down to one syllable if possible. After all, callers know who they are calling. They just need confirmation they have reached the right number. *"XYZ Good Morning"* said cheerfully will do. When did you last review your response to outsiders?

Some other phrases to be avoided might include: *"Sorry, he's in a meeting"*. What the caller wants to know is when will he be **out** of his meeting so he can call back or decide whether to leave a message. *"I'm sorry, Mr Smith is in a meeting until 1.30; can I take a message or would you like to call back?"* Does this sounds more like good service with a caring attitude?

Similarly, it is amazing how many times one is greeted with; *"Mr Fraser is not in his office"*. Again, callers need to know **when** he will be available.

A suggested improvement may be : *"Mr Fraser is not at his desk at the moment, can I put you through to his secretary or can I take a message?"* Of course, the very best thing of all would be if Mr Fraser would set an example in customer care and tell his telephonist if he has had to leave his telephone for any length of time, and when he will be back, so callers can be told **exactly,** and a measure of service provided.

- **IDEA**: Get a friend to call your company when you are out and ask for you, to see how the enquiry is handled. Do it frequently using different people and report back to the person who answers the telephone, not as a reprimand, but to help improve and impress upon them how important a good response is.

A final example...
*"Good morning, XYZ".*
*"Oh good morning, could I speak to Mr Williams please?"*
*"Yes of course, can I say who's calling?"*
*"Colin Rees from Quest Consultants."*
*"Just one moment Colin....."*.

Treating a caller like a long lost friend through the use of the first name is dangerous and discourteous in the extreme. It might be the Chairman of ICI calling your Managing Director to place a record-breaking order, **you** do not know.

Avoid first name familiarity unless you have a relationship with the caller. These examples demonstrate symptoms of poor service and could offend sensitive callers even though your member of staff may think they are acting correctly. Customers, prospects and suppliers all require special treatment and a professional attitude in all dealings with customers will always be noticed. It is not a crime for a telephonist to be friendly and cheerful however bored they may be.

### *Good service can vastly increase your profits through repeat sales over a longer period and costs nothing*

It is likely that you rarely telephone your business to be put *'on hold'*. This means, you might not listen frequently to the *'music'* that your caller endures while waiting for connection. Good customers who telephone to speak with you often can be annoyed by incessant rendering of an electronic version of *'Home on the range'* played three or four times through.

The Swiss glockenspiel is probably worse and these options may not fit the image of your firm. You could decide to turn it off and replace the function with your telephonist frequently informing callers of the state of the call and providing personal, friendly options, or ask BT to provide a replacement.

If your telephonist *'doubles'* as receptionist greeting visitors, ensure that visitors are *'processed'* in a professional and caring manner. I well remember introducing myself at reception, hearing the call put through to inform the secretary of my arrival and being asked to take a seat. It transpired later, the secretary contacted was the wrong one.

Fifteen minutes later, I checked to find that the person I was visiting had forgotten our meeting, and was out. During the fifteen minutes, the person on reception had not checked progress with the secretary but had been playing a computer game in between taking calls. What sort of impression does that portray to visitors, and again, you don't know who they are or how important they are to your company. Management control **is** vital in this area so often thought unimportant.

**IDEA**: Have you received any testimonial letters from customers saying how well you did? The reception area wall is the very best place for that, not the board room or the filing cabinet. Visitors will be impressed with your company even before they meet you. They look even more impressive if they date back ten or twenty years suggesting continuing good service.

If you are expecting a visitor at a pre-determined time, and they arrive on time, see them on time. They have taken the trouble to travel to see you at your office and it is the height of discourtesy to keep them waiting, even for five minutes. Their time is valuable too, even if they are a supplier.

Try to make sure your staff live through one full day without using the phrases *'no problem'*, *'there you go'*, *'cheers'*, and *'speak to you soon'*. Such language becomes **immensely** irritating when exposed to it day in, day out and a lack of imagination in speech can build a perception of lack of creativity or *'stereotyping'* in the business.

If you are going to claim that you provide *'good service'* in your promotions, it has to permeate all layers of the business from top to bottom. This demands a thorough examination of all your procedures wherever there is contact between customers and the staff who deal with people outside your business. This is well worth an investment of time.

## SUMMARY

- If anyone in your company offers poor service, it is probably your fault.

- Meticulous attention to detail and a caring attitude towards those you serve will result in a higher level of service and greater profits from satisfied customers who continually return.

- Prepare an organised disputes procedure so that whenever a customer is let down, positive action is taken.

- Make sure your disputes procedure leads to recovery of the account, not just customer appeasement.

- Make complaint rectification an immediate procedure. There is nothing more annoying that the feeling the supplier has more important things to do that *'deal with me'*.

- An improved customer care policy is useless if only half your staff are performing properly.

- Check your switchboard regularly. Poor initial handling can put a customer in a bad frame of mind and they may not tell you of the experience. A productive customer needs to be *'happy'* to be *'sold to'*.

- When you leave your desk, think about your customers and make it easy for everyone to find you quickly.

- Look around your reception area in the heat of the day. Are you really satisfied with how it looks? Will visitors be impressed? Are they being dealt with, not properly, but really well? Are your testimonial letter hanging straight in their frames?

*Customer care that is 'second to none' reaps its own rewards*

## BUDGET

*What level of budget do you need to reach your set objective?  Promotion should be investment, not expenditure, because it will return in net profit if the promotion is conducted properly. In cases where an improvement is needed, an investment budget is required. You do **not** need to allocate more to obtain improved results.*

A starting point for promotional expenditure in the year to come can be achieved in two ways. The first is to take 10% of net profit from the previous year as the promotional budget.  The other measure generally accepted is between 2% - 5% of turnover as a reasonably affordable starting budget. The level you allocate depends on the size of your turnover, overall resources and anticipated aims.  A small business will need a higher percentage to get going.

This figure is adjusted to the additional sales required for that year against the previous year. If you need a 2% increase in sales this year, add 2% by either method to your promotional budget. This can only be a guide, as the business you are in, the factors affecting selling into your market, and your own company economy are individual items which can affect the level of funds you need.

Ideally, you would take time to decide the detail and cost of the activities in the marketing plan, adding a contingency for the level of sales expansion you require.

***In almost all cases, re-allocating the present budget to be more effective by using it properly in a planned way can be enough to produce a measure of improvement.***

It is an objective of this book to demonstrate that by running promotions in a better way, results can improve without increasing the promotional budget. Spending more on any item reduces net profit and the objective in all things *'marketing'* is to make more, not less. However, capturing more sales does demand a higher budget and it becomes vital to allocate it wisely.

Ascertaining the success or failure of a campaign is often mis-judged. Response should take into account the ongoing sales each new customer will produce over a long period rather than only the turnover directly attributable to each single campaign.

Remember, promotional budget should be *'investment'* not *'expenditure'*.  To be used effectively, it returns as increased net profit, but it is all too common for a business to give up too soon.  One advertisement in the trade press will not bring in floods of new customers - it takes time.

Allocated wisely and monitored properly, promotional expenditure improves the bottom line, and increases market share where it might have been lost.

## MONITORING

*Any promotional activity which is not monitored to produce accurate results afterwards, is better not to have been undertaken in the first place. How else can you decide whether or not to refine it and try again?*

If a promotion ran well, it is vital to know why. If results were only *'average'* and you are aware of the costs and the results exactly, you can assess the worth of allocating further budget to improve on that result when you repeat it. The second time, you can see directly what effect the further increase has.

- **IDEA**: Look at any advertising you may have planned in the next month. Make up a chart with the name of the paper, the space and production cost and the week it is to appear. Allow for three extra columns to add figures of responses over the next three weeks from that advertisement.

*(There is a self help form in the appendix to help you.)*

- **IDEA:** Look at the last advertisement you ran and see if you can construct a coupon at the bottom for readers to respond to you. This might take the form of sending for *'more details,'* your brochure, or a publicity pack or even a free gift for replying. This way, next time you run it, you can see exactly how many people respond to you and from that, you could work out a *'cost per response'* figure.

- **IDEA**: Work out a cost per response figure. Divide the number of responses into the cost of the space. That gives you a comparison of effectiveness against other places you advertise. Now you have a *'benchmark'* of response effectiveness and it becomes possible to measure exactly how good each advertising medium is for your business.

Divide the response columns again so you can **see** the net profit that came directly from those responses. That will show you the return over those weeks against the cost. This system will put you in a much better position to judge whether to commit expenditure to that promotion next time.

When you devise a monitoring system, tie it back to your marketing plan so that results from each promotion can show clearly where more budget could be allocated to better effect. Use the results of promotions to improve sales performance and put budget where it can be most effective.

How many people place advertisements in trade magazines month after month and never attempt to find out who responded to them?

## LOYALTY SCHEMES

*If you accept the fact that a certain level of customers are lost from your business each year, it is obvious that it is vital to keep the customers you have as well as continuing to attract new ones. This section tells you how to keep those hard-won customers.*

It should be said immediately that the best loyalty scheme of all is consistent, good, cheerful, professional service and perceived good value, but in recent years, there has been a significant increase in formal customer loyalty schemes. Retailing in the UK is led by supermarkets and sheds. These businesses allocate huge budgets to attract customers and keep them. Many of their schemes and ideas can be adapted and applied to a smaller, commercial environment.

There is a cost to your business in attracting every new customer, an investment lost if they go to a competitor. Imagine how much profit your best customer produces in one year. Work it out over five years, and then ten. That total becomes the possible loss to you if they are lured to a competitor.

So how can you prevent that situation? A properly instituted customer loyalty scheme ensures that your customers do not form part of the average you might lose this year and it is worth allocating just some of the extra profit they will bring you to extend their purchasing life.

The loyalty scheme should be based on the customer achieving a certain level of business before the benefit is given. If possible the benefit should be redeemable against your own range of goods which have been bought at a wholesale cost. Thus, the customer, working at retail price level, is satisfied with the benefit, and your business benefits since the customer's '*gift*' is at cost.

Customer loyalty schemes should run over long periods to maximise the benefits to the business and keep the customer interested but they require very careful planning to ensure that the rewards offered are substantial enough to keep customers and reasonable enough to protect margins without giving too much away.

**<u>CAUTION</u>**:     You must be mindful that the loyalty reward you extend may not be approved by the company to whom your loyalty scheme is introduced. Some firms adopt the policy that any reward should go to the company, usually in improved discount, rather than to an individual. A personal voucher or gift is sometimes seen as a form of bribery.

Always check each customers' policy before launching your scheme.

- **IDEA**: What type of scheme could you employ? A first scheme might be centered on cards where a stamp is put in a square for every £5 spent. When there are 20 stamps, your customer can choose to continue to collect towards a higher level or accept a voucher. You can send out the stamps with each delivery. Generally, people like to collect things and watch their assets grow, and they share the information with others.

- **IDEA**: When setting the level at which you will reward your customer, make sure it is above the average level of spend as this increases sales and profits with no effort or cost.

Another variation might involve getting a local printer to print up some vouchers. When so many vouchers have been *'earned'* the customer receives maybe £10's worth of gift tokens. These might be your own or some from the High Street. Alternatively, you could use peel-off stickers for the same purpose.

Some *'points'* schemes entail producing a full colour catalogue of available prizes to claim against certain levels of points. Some form of card/stamp collection scheme holds the dual benefit of on-going loyalty as well as allowing *'spot'* rewards such as *'double stamps'* to increase sales on certain items.

- **IDEA**: It is possible to team up with a larger organisation to offer your customers a more substantial reward for their loyalty. Argos stores operate the *'premier'* card scheme where customers from your business earn points from buying your products, redeemable in their stores. The customer can earn points at other participating outlets, as well as yours, and this holds added value. The more businesses which participate, the more points can be awarded. It assists you by providing a full colour Argos gift catalogue which, if you operated a scheme like this on your own, you would have to fund.

You may choose an easier loyalty scheme such as an automatic x% off all purchases over a fixed level spent. This form of loyalty plan helps to increase spending per customer if the level is set correctly, as well as encouraging customers to spend with **you** again rather than with a competitor. This sort of scheme works well and can be seen in various discount catalogues with special gifts for large orders to encourage people to spend more.

The role of your staff in any scheme is paramount to its success. Role playing sessions can help to perfect your loyalty scheme, as well as providing a training and motivation opportunity. In one recent scheme with a client, orders taken by well briefed telephone staff were probably responsible for increasing at least 50% of purchases up to the £50 level.

*Loyalty scheme customers will stay with you, spend more with you,*
*and impede your competitor's sales levels.*

To be effective, such schemes need to last at least three months with a cut off date in case planning mistakes have been made.

One member of a buying group took part in a loyalty programme which was offering M & S vouchers worth £5 over a certain level of purchase. He misread the instructions and offered his customers the voucher on all orders without the qualifying levels, thereby losing considerable face with customers and colleagues when the scheme had to be stopped after just a few weeks.

What will competitors do as soon as they see your loyalty scheme working? Probably institute their own. To counter this, you should add value. One way would be to extend special offers for loyalty scheme customers on presentation of their card.

In marketing circles it has long been felt that creating a 'club' atmosphere can have many beneficial effects. Loyalty schemes isolate a section of your customers who effectively form a *'club'*. As a result, you have the opportunity to make special sales propositions to that captured group.

- **IDEA**: Loyalty customers could be sent an interesting **newsletter** packed with special offers, just for those *'members'*. This makes them feel superior to the casual customer and gives your sales graph a healthy, upward sales rise every time it goes out.

- **IDEA**: Consider a cheese and wine **evening** where all goods are available at 10% off. If you are in an industry where you sell to businesses but your products are of interest to individuals such as stationery, this could work well. It has the side benefit of establishing and *'rewarding'* those relationships.

- **IDEA**: You might consider invitations to special events such as a pre-sale evening with special bargains for privileged customers. Displays and lectures on certain subjects applicable to your business also work well. In a competitive situation, this would add value.

- **IDEA**: Offers from another business are a possibility. Once you have your loyalty scheme in place, team up with other businesses so that both benefit. Is there anyone around in a non competing commercial area who could join forces with you, to increase loyalty for each organisation? Obviously, this is good for both businesses and cements loyalty to both.

An example from the retail sector of this form of networking came when TESCO teamed up with B & Q. If you buy over £10's worth of DIY goods in B & Q, you get two TESCO points on the TESCO club card, redeemable at TESCO. Why do you think they decided to call it a *'club card'* if it wasn't to foster a *'togetherness'* factor?

Loyalty schemes can influence the smallest purchases. If one outlet offers a loyalty bonus and another does not, research shows, the company with the scheme will invariably win the business. One commercial client who needed to recapture a particular segment of the market used the following promotional scheme to excellent effect. Although it started life as a database marketing exercise, it became a long term loyalty scheme.

**CONVERTING THE CHERRY PICKERS**

He sorted his customers into four groups, one of which he called *'cherry pickers'*. These were a group of customers who used his products when they were the best price but had no particular affiliation to him, or indeed to any one supplier, although they had the buying power to divert all their purchasing to him, away from competitors. The object was to use an incentive to persuade as many of them as possible to buy **only** from his business during the scheme. Having experienced his good service and superior quality, it was hoped they would become regular purchasers.

The companies selected for conversion were telephoned, each MD told what was proposed and asked if they minded their staff participating. This presented a sales opportunity in itself. In this case, full communication was an important factor. The promotion was very simple.

*This is how the scheme worked:*
- Each customer was set a turnover target of an average of £1000 a month, having identified this sector as regularly producing an average of £700 per month per customer.

- Each customer was told that on reaching the target, their company would gain an additional 1% discount across the board and a complimentary teddy bear would be sent to the contact. These had proved popular gifts in previous promotions. Their name would go in a hat for a quarterly draw to produce 2 tickets for dinner on the Seine in Paris. Runners up who *'qualified'* received a bottle of Champagne by way of a *'thank you'*.

- Each MD of the qualifying companies received a bottle of Champagne as a *'thank you'* which proved a goodwill earner, raising the profile of the client above his competitors.

- Participating customers were presented with opportunities to boost their turnover with special product promotions, some arranged with manufacturers prior to the event.

In the first six months over 300 customers *'qualified'* usually in excess of the target set. The net gain in turnover directly attributable to the promotion was £57,000 against a cost of around £3000. At the time, Eurostar were providing return tickets to Paris for £69.

These customers were targeted as having the option to change suppliers easily and this promotion was a huge success. His list of cherry picking clients is now half as long.

As the scheme did so well, it was continued for a further six months with slight upward adjustments to the targets, converting it from a promotion to a loyalty scheme.

- **IDEA**: Could your company mount a loyalty scheme to keep those reliable, producing customers you fought so hard to get? What sort of scheme would work best for your customers? What are your objectives in increased sales from customers who continually return to buy from you?

- **IDEA**: Some of the most successful schemes are based around this principle where 2, 3 or even 4 *'levels'* persuade customers to go a little further with you in their buying. Everything they buy from you will not be bought elsewhere and so you are restricting your competitors profitability while extending yours.

## SUMMARY

- Good ideas can often be found in your local supermarket, shed, or other multiple outlet. Some organisations spend thousands each year maximising their sales and profits. Although their retail bias may at first sight seem not to provide anything relevant, consider ways of adapting the principles to your business.

- Who will you offer your loyalty scheme to?

- How will they become eligible?

- What will their benefit be, can you construct a tiered reward?

- How long will it last, who will be in charge of it?

- What results do you expect in added revenue?

- Did you get those results, therefore can you refine it for the next period? Have you got your next idea planned before you launch this one?

## MANUFACTURERS, HOW CAN THEY HELP?

*Generally in Britain, 45% of the shared budget allocated by commercial manufacturers to distributors and retailers is not taken up. The reason? People just do not think to ask.*

Most manufacturers allocate amounts from their marketing budget to spend in conjunction with dealers on joint promotions. Look at the products on your shelves. Which manufacturer hasn't helped your business towards its current objectives lately? Manufacturers often have brochures and leaflets to give away that might help your company to sell more.

### *The more you tell, the more you sell.*

If you have a database of prospects you want to convert to new customers, or a list of customers you want to '*sell up*' to, the chances are that you possess a valuable asset with which to encourage manufacturers to mount a joint promotion with your business. Most manufacturers will supply their promotional leaflets for a joint campaign.

- **IDEA**: You may already have a list of prospects you wish to convert to customers. A manufacturer will not sell direct and therefore would not have a valuable end user list. In general, renting a list costs around £80 - £100 per 1000 names and addresses so this can be an opportunity to prepare a newsletter to send to your list or a list of local businesses you can compile from Kelly's directory, with the manufacturer sharing the costs.

- **IDEA**: Ask for some additional discount or free product at the same time. Sometimes, a manufacturer finds this way to help you better than an allocation of cash, although leaflets or display material will be available as well.

- **IDEA**: Could this be an opportunity to raise the level of prospect customer you target? Dun and Bradstreet top 10,000 UK companies directory listing is available for reference at most large libraries, if you want to aim high.

- **IDEA**: Go down to the warehouse or stockroom and take a look around to see which manufacturer you may be able to approach for promotional support. This tactic can be especially useful when your business suffers a sudden competitive onslaught.

It takes just one call to the Marketing or Managing Director at Head Office. The Representative may be a good source of information so discuss promotional support with him first. However, he has no control over budgets. Secure better terms for a period, ask what promotional plans they have coming up which could help you, ask for money to mount a joint campaign.

# INNOVATION

*How innovative is your business seen to be? Is there a problem in your business which can be overcome by radical thought? The best way to get your business noticed is to be unusual.*

Not much is unique in business life. If you use unusual ways to promote your activities, people will become more aware of you.

If you cannot describe yourself as innovative or creative, that is a sign that you could use the services of a marketing person whose job is to create innovative schemes to improve his clients' sales.

What could you do to add value to your product or service to become more noticeable to consumers? Could you mount a simple promotion to build brand or company awareness?

- **IDEA**: Here's an example of innovative thinking. If you happen to hear that a close rival has *'gone down'*, call BT and ask to take on his telephone number. All the people who were calling him will go through to you. This might include an irate creditor or two but that will be far outweighed by customers, prospects and people who might have seen advertisements or those replying to directory entries placed by the demised business.

- **IDEA**: Innovation in your product mix may help your sales. You could examine what **else** you might sell to customers apart from the normal products they know you supply. So many small business people do not take the time, or have the knowledge to promote in a planned way, which does not maximise effectiveness. See if you can plan to provide your present customers with a new product range and give them a *'trial discount'* to persuade them to try it.

**ADDING INNOVATION.**

Many innovative ideas from the retail sector can be adapted to fit commercial, business to business selling. What counts is how you convert them to your best advantage.

Take the example of a simple sale, a January or Summer event perhaps. There is a difference between putting some posters in the window and placing some advertisements to tell people that your best offers of the year are now available. Careful planning towards achieving an objective is the principle of good marketing.

The following example is from a business in Melbourne that sells men's clothes. It is a small store and carries an exclusive range of European clothes for those who can afford them and who wish to be different. It is the sort of shop where a loyalty scheme would be unnecessary as customers come back anyway, spending thousands of dollars at each visit.

In January, in tune with most other retailers, the shop has a sale. But this sale is phenomenal in terms of results and is due to well planned, skillful marketing. The first task is to check when competitors' sales start. Posing as a potential customer, each is telephoned. The Melbourne store starts one week before anyone else's. Six days before the sale is due to start, 500 letters are sent to all customers outside the designated mailing area who have spent more than a certain amount that year. It reads;

> *Dear valued customer,*
>
> *Our store is having its annual sale starting Monday. For the next three days only, you are invited to visit us anytime between 9.00 am and 9.00 pm. Show us this letter and we will give you 10% off anything you purchase. Plus, you get first pick of what's on offer because you are such a good customer.*

This is the clever bit. It goes on to say that this offer is not open to anyone, only selected, valued customers and it is only available during those six days, of the pre sale week - remember, the sale hasn't started yet.

In those three days, the shop will clear the equivalent of a whole month's takings. During this time, a leaflet is sent to 48,000 *potential* customers in the close suburbs. They come from local electoral lists and live in the area and enjoy three days pre sale specials.

Next to appear is the first newspaper advertisement five days before the start of the sale and radio is booked for the same time in support. The advertisement will focus on the fact that the store provides low priced, European fashion not obtainable anywhere else, their USP and recipients have the chance to enjoy these goods before the official start date. Two weeks after the first newspaper advertisement, the second appears, effectively just towards the end of the two week sale period.

By using this combination, thousands of dollars worth of clothes are sold and most customers believe they are privileged to be the only beneficiary of the offer. This retains the *'personal service'* element and corners some market share well before the competitors.

The sale takes place twice a year and together with an excellent financial achievement, many new customers are attracted to the store and become regular new customers all year round. Local people are not excluded as posters are displayed locally to advertise the event.

It is clear from this example that careful planning, combined with innovative thought can produce significant results. Most growing businesses would think that using advertising alone to tell people of the existence of the sale would be enough and sales would follow. In this case, the proprietor chose a mix of staged mailings, advertising, radio and PR to maximise the opportunity.

Last year, that shop took in excess of $200,000 turnover in 2 weeks and stock was especially imported for the sale, with end of stock lines also cleared.

- **IDEA**: There is no reason why a commercial company could not have a January sale. Invite *'clients'* to come and view the sale stock before it starts. Officially *'mark down'* some loss leaders and take orders for other items at the same time. Just think of the PR value of such an event? How innovative can you be in maximising your sale time? Do you even have a sale?

- **IDEA**: One commercial stationer has an event at Christmas with cheese and wine and tells of the high sales that have come from those evenings. It may well be worth trying this idea whatever business you are in.

*Innovation in your product mix may help your business.*

- **IDEA**: You could examine what else you might sell to customers to make up a special *'package'* of products which, grouped together, sell for a discounted overall price. In this way, more is sold and the customer thinks they have a bigger discount as a result.

### SUMMARY

- Decide how you could boost your profits with a January sale, targeting the different market areas.

- If you run a sale or any event which attracts prospects, find a way to record the name and address of all who come for future use. The Chapter on database marketing suggests ideas on how to use that data.

- Look at the last promotion you did and see if you can re-plan it to add innovation. Use the examples in this section and adapt them for your use.

## SELLING UP

*Selling more to customers you already have is one fast way to increase turnover and profits, costing only a little thought. How many times can you remember hearing a customer express surprise on discovering you stock a certain product they did not realise you carried? As a reason for losing a sale, this happens all the time.*

Selling up takes different forms, the first is selling more to people who already buy from you, that is more of the usual product range, the second extends them further towards the goal of purchasing all your products. The objective is to make you the sole supplier for everything in that field. Your present customers already know you and are aware of your good service so selling **more** to them should not be so difficult or costly.

If you receive an order, try to *'sell up'* the quantity. You could do that by offering a discount for a larger number. Are there any products that 'go with' the product your customer orders? Pens and paper, trucks and trailers, machinery and spare parts, each presents a selling up opportunity.

The natural progression from there would involve a conversation such as; *"We have been supplying our 'x' product to you for some time now. You know our service and quality are good, would you like us to supply a trial order on product 'Y' on the same terms?"* In each case, using the fact that they are buying from you presents an opportunity to sell more.

Sometimes, a loyal customer buys elsewhere. He doesn't know, or **think** you stock the desired item because it is different from the range he normally purchases.

Naturally, it is imperative for sales staff to be vigilant, aware of customer purchases and to be informed about your entire product range. It is not enough to send out an annual or discount catalogue with all the lines in it, as that pre-supposes they read it or use it other than when they refer to it with a need.

But having sent it, by talking to them about it, highlighting sections and asking questions, more will be sold and customers slowly educated to know exactly what you do provide, rather than what they expect to be available from your company. The computer can be used to tell you which customers buy which ranges. It is then possible to undertake a special sales thrust *'selling up'* to them.

- **IDEA**: Why not run a special promotion offering discounts on your **least** known products in order to educate your customers as to the extent and scope of the range of products you handle.

## PRICE PERCEPTION

*If your customers perceive your company as 'expensive', what can you do about it? How should you present your prices to protect your reputation and margins while retaining your customers' business?*

The marketing skill required is one that enables the customer to perceive that your price is good and holds value for them although possibly, it is not the very best offer if they were to shop around. It is necessary to *'win the mind of the customer'* towards seeing your company as a place which represents consistent value.

A well-constructed positioning statement will ensure that the *'perceived value'* of your goods is low. This is further supported by the way you display your prices in leaflets, advertisements, brochures and at the point of sale. It takes time and creative thought to achieve a good result although it costs hardly anything to achieve.

The problem with pricing is being able to show your customer a price that they will perceive as reasonable but at the same time, makes you a good margin. A commercial company with a promotional leaflet or brochure faces the same problems as the retailer with customers walking round a showroom.

In this context, pricing statements and how you display prices become very important. A commercial business displays prices promotionally by way of an advert, a discount brochure, a leaflet or a mailer. If you are prospecting, looking for new customers, you will not gain new business if your prospect believes your prices to be higher than his present supplier. Consequently, prospecting material in particular must carry very competitive overall pricing.

The way you show prices is very important. To take an example of an office desk and chair set which you have reduced in a promotion, how could this best be portrayed? If the price was originally £425 and you reduce it to £340, how should you show it, to demonstrate the significance of the reduction to the customer?

If you display the lower price alone, you can not be sure that your customers will know that £340 is a good price. You need to show both prices and emphasise the saving rather than expect the customer to work it out mentally.

The most noticeable way in a discount brochure, flyer or POS card, is to show a % discount saving that customers or prospects can recognise quickly as a really good offer.

The following example shows three ways that the reduction might be presented to customers.

**NOW ONLY £340**

**SAVE £85**
**WAS £425,**
**NOW £340**

Just £340 with
# 20% OFF!!
Reduced from £425
*FOR 10 DAYS ONLY*

In the second example, you attract more attention by use of a *'flash'* to say "SAVE £85." You are beginning to show the customer value he can readily understand. The third suggestion is the most powerful, enhanced with exclamation marks. It is easy to see from these examples how many ways there are to display the same message and you must chose the method best suited to your customers. Asking them is one way to find out for sure.

- **IDEA**: Wherever possible, put a time limit on the offer. It suggests this is *'not for ever'* and provokes an earlier buying decision

**HELP HINT:** Choose a way to display all your pricing that will be simple, easily understood and provides the best reflection of the promotion value.

**CAUTION**: It is better to be creative and use as many phrases as possible to provide the customer with a *'perceived value'* idea. The words *'only'* and *'just'* should be used with caution when describing a price. It is tempting to show *'only'* before every price. By the time your customer is just part way through your discount brochure or round your showroom, it will become irritating. Put the word *'only'* away from the price as in the examples below.

*Special Offer! £2.99*               *Efficiency reduction, £2.99*
*Super value price £2.99*            *XYZ special price, £2.99*
*Red Hot Special, just £2.99*        *Only this week, £2.99*
*Low price, only here £2.99*         *Fantastic saving £2.99*

Seen recently on a market fruit stall: *"Carrots, 2lbs. for 70p."* Seen on another stall: *"Carrots, 40p a lb"*. Given the choice a customer is persuaded to buy the 2lbs option on price and because, with a good sign, the stall holder has suggested better value from the 2lb purchase. It is likely that most customers would perceive this value. How could you apply this thinking to your products?

**HELP HINT**: Look at a copy of your latest leaflet, mailer, brochure or catalogue and study the way you have presented your prices. Are you really doing everything possible to **sell** your goods or are you just **presenting** them?

## SUPPLIERS

*How many business people take their suppliers for granted?   This section serves as a guide to increasing profits by 'fostering' relations with suppliers.*

It is well known there is more than one way to make more profit.  One way is to sell more at the right margin. Another is to save more cost wherever you can and a good supplier can help to achieve this for you.

Why then do we treat suppliers so badly?  Some MD's are so distracted by their own power that if a supplier makes a suggestion, it is met with an automatic, negative reaction. Treating suppliers properly means allowing them to work closely with you as external members of your team.  Admittedly, they have to earn that right, but they can be extremely helpful, because they want to be.

Getting close to suppliers as people and fostering a strong business relationship can cement what is often a foolproof association resulting in fine work, great ideas, reasonable costs, good support and occasionally, a real spark of initiative.  In one case I know of, although never admitted, such a relationship led to the launch of a new product the company believed they may not have thought of.

Therefore, it is inadvisable to treat suppliers badly as they will not give of their best. They are running a business too and you have to let them make some profits, or they won't be there to help you.

Good suppliers are willing to offer advice on various technicalities of their business, even when there is no work there for them.  Often they are willing to work an evening or weekend to complete a difficult job.  They will keep to the estimate to retain your goodwill, even in instances where the project turns out to be more than was thought at commencement.  You will still point out areas with which you are unhappy and you will find they are corrected quickly. You should pay suppliers quickly as this makes your business truly valuable to them, enhancing the relationship. You should enjoy a good standard of work and service as a result.

In turn, your clients should receive the same standard of service you enjoy, on the elements you sub-contract.  Recently I wrote, prepared and printed 2000 copies of a full colour newsletter for a client in four days, delivered to a conference, printed, dried, stitched and perfect putting myself out considerably, to help that client achieve their objective and strengthen our relationship.  The job was an enjoyable challenge, it was profitable, and my efforts were appreciated.

**A good relationship with a reliable supplier can increase your profits.**

## COMPETITORS

*One of the biggest problems facing a small business is the threat of being swamped by a competing big business. If you are forced to compete with a large competitor, this chapter will help.*

Every small company naturally tends to panic when faced with a problem caused by a big budget competitor. But in most cases, they probably represent only one tenth of the threat you perceive.

First, their sheer size brings its own problems. It may well take them months to make a decision to combat something you do, by which time, you are on to the next project. Like a supertanker that takes hours to slow down from full speed ahead, a big company has to involve many people in a decision, often involving meeting after meeting. A strategy might not evolve anyway because it runs out of momentum.

They may not be bothered by you because the effect you can have on them may be minimal. It's all too much trouble and they plan their marketing months, sometimes years ahead.

The real difficulty is that the small business person is on their own. Often, there is no one with whom to discuss a problem. It is easy to take fright when you see your entire living under threat with the mortgage, the rent, and the overdraft at risk. Yet competition can sometimes be an opportunity if you can investigate the source of your opponent's mistake. Remember, their customers are drifting away each year as will yours if nothing is done to keep or replace them.

It is just as easy to become concerned about the threat of competitors in a medium sized business, probably worse, as you all sit around the table talking yourselves into a diabolical situation, often based on emotive feeling rather than actual fact. The end result is an agreement to give up.

Most markets are under-supplied and there's room for both of you to find the right niche. The trick is to provide your products better and faster, not necessarily cheaper.

Often, a growing business which is threatened spends time agonising over what *might* happen. Invariably, there is plenty of business in any market place that the big players really do not want as it is unprofitable for them. Their sights are set on very large accounts that can be easily serviced at a good margin rather than smaller accounts where the margin is less.

The answer is to treat the problem as a science. Competing is an intelligent form of battle and an intellectual challenge where no one gets killed. Study exactly what the competition does and how they do it. Where are they advertising this month? What are they saying to their prospects? How does it effect what you are doing and your priorities?

Do you have a major competitor on the doorstep that you wish was not there? Have you really studied that competitor to see where his weaknesses are and where you might gain a foothold?

As an example, imagine there is a company three times your size not 100 yards from you, stocking the same products as you do and at 10% less than your prices. Matching his prices cuts your margins. In precisely this situation, a marketing person will look for ways to add value to your product or service which effectively gives your customers more for their spend and so endears them to you against your competitor. This situation makes USP's critical.

**HELP HINT**:   If you find yourself in that position, look at your competitor's staff.  Are they mainly students and part-time workers?  How good is the advice he can give his customers compared with that which your full-time, trained staff can provide?  That is the message you must get across to your customers and prospects. First, find the weakness.

- **IDEA**: Watch what the competition is up to.  Where are they, what are they saying, where do they think their priorities are? They could be the same as yours so you need to show extra benefits.

**HELP HINT**:    In terms of a local audit, list all the competitors in your area, in order of threat to you, the strongest threat first and grade them from 1 - 5 in order of importance. Against each one, write why you think they are a threat - is it their size, promotional spend, pricing, layout, or staff.  Now assess exactly how much of a threat they are in terms of the business they take from you so that you might be able to see the areas of promotion where you need to redress the balance and bring customers to you rather than to them.

Get it on paper and see where to attack the problem. What strengths do you have that they do not?  An example might be as follows:-

- XYZ business:  Much better advertising than us
- Has more staff than we do, more qualified
- Better location, close to a main road.
- Our customers say what nice people they are

In the examples above, as with the SWOT analysis in an earlier chapter, the points put themselves in priority of importance. Looking at advertising, there may well be more you can do about a competitor's big advertising spend without increasing your own budget. Look at the size, extent, content and place where XYZ is advertising.  How can you add value?  Can you put an offer in your advertisements or feature a more popular range?

Which product range is he offering at better prices?  Can you get some manufacturer support for a special promotion just on that range?  Do they advertise every single month or is it every other month and where do they advertise, that might present an opportunity?

Have they changed the advertisement recently because if not, either they are very lazy, or it's working? Is a regular advertisement shrinking in size? What is being offered this month against last month? Is your design and image stronger than theirs?

If the competition stops advertising, then you should ask yourself why? Is it a momentary lapse to recover budget and so a chance for you to gain the advantage or is there more to it than that? Perhaps they are testing alternative media? Much can be learned from monitoring a competitor's exposure. Watch what they do. Which products do they regularly promote as they will be good sellers?

By reallocating your budget, you could make it more effective against them even if you can not increase it. Go through each point where you compete to find the weak spots to attack.

In the example at the bottom of the previous page, you should conduct a customer survey to see what is meant by *"what nice people they are"* and decide what to do to match it.

- **IDEA**: One of the best ways to inform yourself about what your competitor is doing, as well as getting some idea of future plans, is to attend one of their exhibitions. As a member of the public, you present yourself on their stand as a *'punter'*. You will not believe how much the representative will tell you when pumped. He thinks you will buy from him. You lead him on. He wants to impress you with everything he knows about his products and his company's policy and even, their future plans.

- **IDEA**: Every large company is pretty adept at collecting names and addresses, setting up databases and using database marketing techniques to sell more product. Using your home address, buy one of their products which will get your name on to their database. Then, as they execute a promotion, you will receive the details and be well placed to take your own remedial actions.

**HELP HINT**: Competition, especially if it is big, can be of great use to a growing business. Their promotional strength creates a bigger market for you, as well as them. What are they concentrating on at the moment? Where can you jump in, strike, and pull back again? Use their research which costs them millions.

There is an argument for appearing alongside the advertising of a larger competitor with exactly the same product or offer especially if you can add value where they do not. Free delivery is an example. The likelihood of a prospect contacting both suppliers is high. Some customers perceive a small business will provide a more personal service. Ask the magazine to place your advertisement next to theirs as a test and judge if response increases against the times you appear alone.

Yes, competition is a threat to a growing organisation but how might it affect your business? If your business is plagued with heavy competition this could be of assistance to you, as they are effectively spending their budget to create a market which you can infiltrate. If they are *'big'* and you are effectively *'small'*, believe it or not, you have some very distinct advantages.

## SUMMARY

Once a competitor arrives, there is little you can do until they leave apart from securing your market share. Make sure every single customer is regularly communicated with and will not forget you. Service levels throughout your company need to improve and be maintained. Look at the aspect of selling up with ever contact you have with your customers.

If the competitor is a much larger organisation than yours, there will be aspects of their market they do not wish to service. Smaller accounts are more costly for them to service properly and these will form the basis of your marketing activity from now on. Be on the look-out for large accounts who your competitor might have let down as this is a definite entrance for you as you grow.

Watch for the disadvantages of running a large, unwieldy company where staff do not always do as they are instructed and where internal communications are often poor.

- Like a hawk, study every move they make

- Competing is a science not *'disaster recovery'* or *'damage limitation'*. See it as an advantage. Look for the benefits it can bring, not the problems

- Study the way they operate and collect as much on-going information on them as you can

- Attend their next exhibition, use any opportunity to *'chat up'* one of their representatives

- Interview as many of their staff as you can

- Watch for areas in their product range where you can fill a hole or provide an advantage to customers

- Study their advertising

- Get your name on their database

## SELLING

*For those in a profession or service where the 'product' may be hard to define, the selling process can sometimes be clouded in an unpenetratable mystique. To a solicitor or accountant, the sales process is alien. Your personal perception of the average sales person may well be the only factor holding you back. You don't have to enjoy the activity but it brings in more profit.*

As we said in the introduction, selling is what you do when the telephone rings and this book is all about marketing, creating an environment where selling can best take place. But the sales process is not complex and often, success can be achieved from a full knowledge of your product or service, a pleasant personality and a little passion or enthusiasm.

The best selling situation is face-to-face, where you can judge reactions, answer objections and bring the matter to a successful conclusion before you leave. In business to business selling, the marketing methods that follow in this section can achieve that meeting, where needs can be fully assessed and services presented properly, with full understanding on both sides. In such a situation, selling yourself and your sincerity is the first step.

Selling does need not be *'hard nosed'*. The common myth of the double-glazing sales technique may be right for that industry but generally, people do not respond well to a forced approach. The most successful sales people use their personality to sell subtly through questioning, countering objections with positive sales points and gently forming a relationship based on trust. It is then critical to fulfill exactly what you promise.

### *One of the greatest selling skills is listening.*

During the sales conversation, the prospect will be giving a great deal of useful information about his needs, suppliers he has been using and their areas of weakness, requirements that he has as an individual. You will be asking questions to provoke that information, watching for areas where you can fulfill those needs or service the account in a better way, presenting your sales points when the time is right and waiting for the buying signals that will allow you to close the sale.

If you are in front of the correct person, anyone can achieve that. There are really no hard and fast rules about human relationships although there are things one should, and should not do, so it is in selling. Convincing someone to buy from you is a gradual process of instilling trust, persuading that person you are the best at what you do and that above all, his trust will be rewarded with on-going good value service.

If the prospect has granted you an *'audience'* he must be interested. You have one opportunity. Plan and be confident for tomorrow, **you** could sell. The following chapter will help the process.

CHAPTER 3

## MARKETING METHODS

*The previous chapter dealt with the plans you should make before launching a promotional programme. A strong foundation must be laid and the aims and policies implemented to produce profits. **Preparation and planning is vital**, so is employing USP's and wherever possible, using your positioning statement and this applies to **all** the methods.*

In this chapter, I will consider twenty three marketing methods you can use to promote your business. The articles are designed for you to be able to adopt the method from day one. You do not need to consult an expert to teach you how to sell on the telephone, mail or advertise; the guidelines are here.

You will probably be advertising already so I will assume you know the basics, and I will try to give you a guide as to how and where you might get better results for the same budget.

The other methods may be ones you have heard of but know little about. As you consider each one, apply the thinking to your business and evaluate results. You need to be comfortable with the rudiments of how to achieve the objective, and you should establish a monitoring programme early on.

If you fail the first time, do not give up; reformulate and try again. So many managers expect high results from just one attempt at a method and often decide against using it again if results are poor, claiming *"it didn't work"*. They can never give valid reasons why.

Adjust your approach and test it again. This goes for advertising too. Your consumers will not respond in large numbers just because you advertised once. Your company and products may be the most important thing to you, but you need to capture consumer attention, and keep it while you fulfil their needs. Most schemes **will** work, given time and a reasonable trial period, but you cannot expect to achieve a profitable result overnight even though small business people always expect to.

## THE MARKETING PRINCIPLES

*Just before we look at various ways to create sales, it might be helpful to establish elements that are common to many promotions.*

Whenever a promotion is run, a mailshot, a newspaper advertisement, even a telephone sales call, there are certain elements common to each.

I have said that people buy when they have a need and so any promotion should be geared towards creating or suggesting a need that your product or service might fulfill. Only then is it worth carrying on to tell the prospect that you are the best supplier.

A very common mistake in a busy environment is to believe that any promotion is there to sell you, for instance using corporate details as the headline. So often in advertisements and promotions of all sorts, one sees the company name or logo presented first as the most predominant feature. Where bigger companies may indulge in this practice using their well known name to increase market share, smaller growing organisations usually do not have the necessary budget to sustain that activity. Presenting the company as the best place to obtain a product is less important than the product or the need itself, as it is this, people buy.

When deciding what to say, you could follow the simple steps below in planning the text with '*need*' at the forefront of the objective.

ELEMENT 1:     A Headline or statement to capture attention. This is covered in more detail for press advertising in the next section and much of that detail is appropriate with all promotions.

ELEMENT 2:     The body copy or text to explain the need you seek to create and put forward the sales points of the particular product or service you provide. Then describe why that product or service would be better coming from your company rather than a competitor.

ELEMENT 3:     Often termed '*the call to action*', tell your prospects what you want them to do. That does not mean buy from you but send for details, call you, send in a coupon, telephone for a free gift or take the action that leads to your opportunity to close the sale.

ELEMENT 4:     Tell them who you are but most importantly, make it easy for them to reach you. This is the correct place for your appropriate corporate details, logo and positioning statement.

You will refine these ideas according to the method you use but reducing promotions to these elements does simplify understanding of the best way to organise any approach. Getting the elements there, in the right order, may be critical to a good response

## MARKETING METHOD NUMBER 1: ADVERTISING

*Advertising was severely hit during the recession and advertisers reacted in two ways: those who increased advertising spending to retain market share and those who maximised net profitability by reducing the spend. The advertising world believes the former strategy to have been more successful than the latter and although everyone's margins were hit, those who kept consumers aware of their brand managed to keep market share in a declining market.*

To a growing business with a small budget, advertising is not usually the route to a sudden upturn in sales, even though it is increasing consumer awareness. No doubt your industry has a number of trade magazines serving it and trade magazine readers, like all consumers will respond to *'a special offer'*. While most readers are looking for news of their industry, new products and processes, advertising is important in raising and retaining awareness, thus, protecting market share.

Contrary to the opinion of trade press sales staff, the space size makes very little difference in gaining additional response. Response to regular small advertisements, up to three in one issue, will often outweigh that of an advertisement three times larger. The way to find out is to test and monitor until the best formula is found.

It is important not to risk funds that your business cannot afford on grandiose schemes prepared without thought, where it is difficult to gauge a result. Most of the trade press people are singularly unhelpful in making suggestions on how best to advertise, as their skill is selling space, not designing advertisements.

In fairness, they cannot know much about your company or products and would be ill-advised to offer advice. The mechanics of how to fill the space does not figure in their training. They are good at providing statistics and readership profiles. The mere suggestion that you might spend money with them will yield a full media pack and samples of back issues from any magazine that you may think relevant.

It is common when time is pressing to place an advertisement, probably on a special space offer, and then forget it. However, if your headline does not capture reader attention, and if the advertisement has not been properly thought through with due regard to the market being addressed and the needs of that market, then you will not maximise the response. That means you lose profit.

## MEDIA BUYING

*If you are placing the odd advertisement in the trade press occasionally, there is little point in formalising your media buying arrangements. However, if you are buying larger amounts of space in a year, you could obtain benefit from using a media buying house.*

If you advertise infrequently and place the space yourself be sure to ask for some kind of discount. Advertising agencies enjoy between 10 - 15% discount so you can obtain that at least. Sometimes, you will be asked to pay in advance but if it gets you more discount depending how you are managing your cashflow, it could be worth it. Spot placing means you have to take space when it is available and so your campaign is unplanned but usually, less expensive.

**CAUTION**: Watch special positions such as inside and outside covers and ear pieces which carry a premium.

**HELP HINT**: Always ask for a high, right hand page which carries the most likely chance to be seen.

If your business uses a great deal of space in local, national media, or radio or if you intend to buy TV airtime, then it may well be in your interest to contact a media buying house. These are companies set up to buy media for their customers and because of the total amount they spend on behalf of all their clients in the course of a year, they are able to buy very cheaply and get the maximum possible discount some of which could come to you.

To maximise the discount, a media buying house will plan a campaign in great detail, providing all the statistics you need, directly from their computer. They will place the space and send you one bill which helps your accounting. Sometimes, if your account is big enough, they will ask you for an annual fee and give you all the discounts they negotiate on your behalf. You have the benefit of their media expertise and volume discounts.

One area where they can help considerably is investigating new media for you that you might not be aware of. They will be able to supply rates and reader profiles and advise you on the best way to use the medium.

### SUMMARY

•     Telephone some media buying firms and ask for their literature.

•     Decide if your annual space expenditure might justify the maximum discount levels.

## COLOUR OR MONO?

*A dilemma: should you spend more budget to make your advertisement full colour?*

It is well known that upgrading to colour in most promotional pieces creates a bigger response. The obvious difference in cost between colour and mono advertisements is due to the use of photographs, and the added cost of the process, which is more complex in colour than in mono.

- **IDEA**: Your decision may be forced by budget considerations but if you think that response could increase, get your studio to prepare a colour advertisement that will work with other promotional pieces such as mailers, leaflets or posters. That way, you will be getting the best value from the colour origination, as the more you use it, the more cost effective it becomes.

The studio will advise you on the best way to use the colour origination more than once and how to alter the text. This can often be accomplished with just a black plate change.

## WHO WILL PREPARE THE ARTWORK?

Once the advertising space is purchased, if you are unsure how to design your advertisement, the magazine will prepare your artwork for you, usually at no cost if you are not too demanding.

All trade magazines employ graphic designers who will put an advertisement together. However, they might use the same typefaces for each advertisement they design and you could find that yours looks quite like the one placed next to it. Having said that, this service **is** free. They will work to whatever brief you give them but they will not know anything about your company, market or customers.

If you prefer to use freelance services for each stage of production rather than letting a design studio do it, be sure to get the correct *'mechanical data'*, that is the right sizes, correct film right/left reading, emulsion up or down, correct screen size and so on. This is a very technical process so be sure you understand what is involved. If this information means nothing to you, it may be best to get a studio or advertising agency involved.

Some years back, our graphic design studio placed eight colour pages for a property client in a *'perfect bound'* trade magazine. When it was published, the text and photographs merged into the spine so that each page did not meet up properly with the facing page and 10% of the content could not be seen. We were not technically aware of the process although the magazine insisted that we had been informed of the need for *'extra bleed'* with perfect binding. To run a double page advertisement across a perfect bound page takes more space than for a double page spread, collated and *'saddle stitched'* (stapled).

Happily, with efficient record keeping and the help of the reproduction house, we were able to prove responsibility was not ours. However, the incident could have yielded us a huge loss with advertising space alone worth some £20k and a client who spent £5000 a year on a legal protection policy.

## ALL ABOUT PHOTO LIBRARIES.

You may decide to hire a photograph from a photo library to enhance your advertisement. This usually involves a search fee **and** a hire fee. Check the fees before you start as it can be expensive.

Picture libraries are in a quandary at present, forced to let technology lead them and provide transparencies on CD. For around £150 each CD can carry 100, unlimited use images in low and high resolution (low resolution is used for visuals, high when they have to be reproduced in the press or a brochure).

You can always ask for mono run-outs of the pictures in the hope that on the disc you want there will be others you can use as, once purchased, the images are yours to use without paying another fee. It is said that some images can be downloaded from the Internet but be cautious about viruses and copyright.

Single transparencies are quite expensive and vary in cost from around £100 to £500 for a single use. The fee depends on the position of your advertisement in the magazine, the circulation, and how rare a photograph is. You can be sure the quality of the image will be excellent.

**HELP HINT**: If you need to use a library picture, haggle hard as it is possible to pay less than the asking cost. At the very least, you should aim to eliminate search fees.

Be aware of new technology which digitises photographs on computer. Last year, we converted four photographs of a modern industrial office estate and three different delivery vans, into a fleet of about 50 vehicles outside modern offices using computer digitisation techniques. The process was required as the client's warehouse was small and on the less up-market side of Stoke-on-Trent. The cost to the client to produce an acceptable photograph this way was £180.

There are two ways to produce a colour advertisement without incurring high costs. One is to ask your design studio who quite legally keep their own photographs from previous work or have their own libraries of pictures they have taken and have never used.

The second method is to prepare a *'duotone'*. This is a mono photograph to which a blend of one colour is added to black to produce a mix. Blue and black work well. The process is quite acceptable for company brochures printed on white stock and can work well on advertisements, depending upon the creativity of your designers.

CAN YOU DESIGN YOUR OWN ADVERTISEMENT?

*If the idea of a design studio or advertising agency is impractical, or if your budget is too small, there are ways you can produce your own 'artwork' but you need to be sure you know what you are doing.*

If your advertisement is prepared professionally, it will be more costly, but of better quality. If you prepare it yourself, you will save budget but will it be successful, how much time will it take and do you have enough technical knowledge to justify the financial saving?

In order to place an advertisement, you buy the space and then produce a bromide or PMT, (photo mechanical transfer), often referred to as '*artwork*', which carries your text in a format from which the magazine can make a printing plate.

You may consider allocating some budget towards effective advertising by employing a specialist. If you want individualism or new ideas, or you are concerned as to the effectiveness of your present strategy, this is the only sensible course of action open to you. You can consult a marketing advisor, advertising agency, freelance graphic designer or a local design studio.

For a simple mono advertisement, you can use your own laser printer if it produces at least 600 dots per square inch and you can print out on special bromide paper.

**HELP HINT**:   Don't use too many typefaces and stick to common ones.  Avoid clipart, the sign of an amateur production.

Most people have a file of ideas from other industries that could be adapted for their use.  Mine is called a '*cribs*' file, borrowing ideas from other areas.  What you call it doesn't matter as long as you take notice of advertising around you and think of possible adaptations to your business.

- **IDEA**: Start a file of your competitors advertising, not to copy it as that will confuse your customer and upset your competitor. Keep advertisements over a period of time to give an insight into your competitor's thinking, how space is used, what is said, how the USP's are presented. This can be immensely helpful when you come to compete.

- **IDEA**: Look at your trade press, other areas and industries, in fact, whenever you read a magazine and see an idea with merit, rush to the photocopier.  Do it immediately or you will not remember.

## WHERE SHOULD YOU ADVERTISE?

*Who to target with your sales message is vital to the success of your advertising. Do you give it the measure of importance it deserves?*

What is the overall purpose of advertising if not to gain sales leads? Admittedly, it does raise awareness, it allows you to talk to people about your product or service which might prompt them to respond to find out more, but these are side benefits. The real aim is to sell.

Are you advertising in the right magazine to address your target market? Often, there are two markets, the target market and the lateral or fringe market. The target market is the obvious or traditional place to offer your product for sale. A fringe or lateral market is a less important, secondary market.

A lateral market is unlikely to yield as many sales as a more defined target market. Where will you stand the best chance to sell the most, profitably? - that is the target market. There is little to be gained from allocating a budget to give you a presence across the board. Far better to concentrate limited resources into the most effective area.

**HELP HINT**:   Research each possibility and select the magazine with the greatest penetration into your market place. Be content to advertise there and monitor response carefully.

**HELP HINT**:   It is surprising how little response results from placing your advertisement in a second trade magazine even though the combined circulation may be increased.

Let us suppose there are three magazines serving your target market. Number one has 60% of the available circulation, the second has 30%, the third has 10%. It is not widely realised that by adding the second option, and so reaching a combined 90% of the total available circulation, usually, this will only result in a few extra responses.

It is possible that the readership of the second magazine in our example represents a more targeted profile of your prospect market even though it has a smaller circulation. While the first one has a bigger circulation, there may not be so many good prospects. That means, in this case, the second is where you should be.

To find out which magazine contains the highest target readership, look at the reader profile issued by the magazine and then put the same advertisement in all the magazines for three months and monitor response. Do it again with a different advertisement for another three months after a gap of, say one month, and see the difference. Wherever possible, use a coupon or voucher and code the advertisement in each paper so that you can be sure of which response came from where. Lastly, draw up a response chart and stick it on the wall to remind you to fill it in after the event. (*See appendix*)

**HELP HINT**: Research, however simple, is important. It is astonishing how many people spend vast sums of their company profits advertising with no research data to work on, and take no account of the response and the amount of gross profit which returned from that campaign. How can they know whether it was a justified expenditure and worth repeating?

> *Many advertisers place one advertisement and believe*
> *new customers will flood in. Don't expect this.*

A minimum campaign run of three advertisements is the least exposure necessary to gain a result. Once you have found a formula that works, stick to it. Marlboro have not altered their general brand image of the *'macho'* male since they started which must mean it works for them. Decide the needs of your target prospects and go directly to that market with your message and positioning statement, remembering that people respond to a need, not to an advertisement.

Are there any magazines in your area you didn't know about? Periodicals are constantly merging. The local Library can help with a reference book known as BRAD, (British Rates and Data). BRAD comes in two sections, one for newspapers, the other for magazines and trade press in the UK. It is published annually and lists every paper by area and magazine by industry.

It gives advertising rates, column sizes, contact telephone numbers and circulation figures. Free newspapers are followed by VFD, others by ABC. These are bona fide, audited figures, not to be confused with *'readership'* which is arrived at by multiplying circulation by 2, 3 or 4 depending on the result required. Full details of how ABC and VFD figures are arrived at are on the inside pages of BRAD.

### LOW COST ADVERTISING SPACE

*It is possible to obtain low cost advertising if you know how to go about it. Of course, these ideas will not suit **all** commercial enterprises but some may benefit.*

- **IDEA**: Try the technique of *'spot'* placing your advertisements. This is a method where you wait with copy in hand until the sales department of your favoured trade magazine calls you in desperation. It is close to their deadline to publish and there is still advertising space unfilled. This is definitely *'silly money'* time and you shouldn't need to spend more than 20% of rate card.

- **IDEA**: One other method might be to send them a bromide of your advertisement and a cheque for say, 40% of the usual page rate, together with a letter saying that if they need a space filler, please use the enclosed. You should find it is published quite soon, and I have known this approach to work with colour advertisements as well if they are already holding your colour separations.

These methods can save hundreds of pounds over placing regular weekly or monthly advertising, even though the use of the advertisement is a little unplanned.

## RADIO ADVERTISING

*It is more expensive but look at the size of the audience you will reach.*

At the local level, radio advertising is designed more for retailers selling to the public, although business-to-business use is not uncommon, especially where commercial and retailing overlap. The only reason you may not use it is because the trade magazines are so much easier, you know how they work and you may not have considered radio which does not suit every product and service.

Assuming that you are in a good consumer catchment area with a willing radio sales team who want you to be successful, radio can bring a significant response.

Radio can be very successful in two areas of marketing. The first is where time is important. Where you need a very fast response such as people to attend a trade function, exhibition or seminar, a radio commercial broadcast a week before can have a dramatic effect on attendance.

The second major use is in building brand awareness. Campaigns typically run for a longer period, say thirteen weeks, during which time a number of spots are allocated to winning customer's minds. However, we have said previously that awareness advertising is often out of reach for a growing business with a smaller budget.

It is common for a radio sales team to provide you with accurate listener data and help in constructing commercials that work. Usually, they are more professional than newspaper sales people. Radio stations invariably offer bonus spots or discounts to first time advertisers, so negotiate hard.

We hear a radio advertisement whether we want to or not. It is on in the kitchen, the car, the bath. We have no choice but to hear it if we are too lazy to use the *'off'* switch between commercials and risk missing half the programme. Radio commercials reach a huge audience in comparison with local papers, and the advertisement can be seasonally adjusted with just a change of copy. Given a catchy jingle which costs anywhere from £500 - £800 to commission, the station will produce a commercial for around £100 and provide a professional voice-over artist.

Give up all thoughts of a *'well known artiste'* to do your voice overs - it is not worth the expense until you have proved the medium works for you and your local station has voice-over professionals available who expect to make your commercial for you anyway.

It is more difficult to gauge response to radio ads as you can not ask people to bring in a voucher or copy of an advertisement. Radio should not mean you dispense with other forms of advertising such as local or trade press either, the best formula is a combination of the two.

• Testing is critical, measure any increase in sales against the same period last year.

• Listen to others in your local Chamber of Commerce, business network or other group to assess what effect radio has had on their business.

## IS TV OUT OF THE QUESTION?

*Not necessarily, but it is a budget risk to a small company.*

The dilemma with any sizeable promotion undertaken by a growing company is in allocating the necessary funding. If this is not available, corners are cut, a second class job results which can have an adverse effect on response. If the promotion does not reach a satisfactory result how does your company sustain promotional activity for the rest of the financial year?

Most TV regions are comprised of separate transmission areas. An example is Anglia which has three separate areas making up the Anglia region. This means a TV commercial can be screened in one, or all these areas which helps where geographical targeting is important. The budget is reduced by a third when one area is selected which means testing can be achieved at relatively low cost.

Some TV stations provide superb discounts to first time advertisers. TV air time works very much on supply and demand. If enough advertisers are queuing for air time, rates against the rate card will be high and visa versa. However, be cautious if your business is located anywhere near a major conurbation, especially London, as these regions charge higher rates due to the large population that their transmission area covers.

Most stations will *'make'* the commercial for you in their studio which saves the cost of hiring a production company and external studio facilities. The cheapest commercial is one which uses slides and a voice-over rather than library film or video footage.

## WHAT SHOULD THE ADVERTISEMENT SAY?

*Having chosen the right medium, what should you say?  Headlines need to stand out, capture attention and target the profiled customer.  How is it done?*

The first direction many managers think of is along the lines of ; *"We're here, come and buy from us"*.  Well, why should people buy from you and not the place down the road?  You must give them a reason.  Is your existence an interesting enough reason for a headline capable of capturing attention?

People buy for two reasons; when they have a need or when they see or hear of something they *'might'* need later but decide to purchase now - an impulse purchase.

You are seeking an opportunity to put forward reasons why customers should buy your product **first** and from **you**, second.  You want to create a need in their mind or give them a reason to buy something on the spur of the moment.  You must make it easy for them to understand what you provide, perceive value, and as important, the process of purchasing must be made easy. You need to describe what is available and close with a call to action, telling them what you want them to do.

Response advertising, where there is a coupon or voucher for people to return is more likely to be effective and will be measurable.  Advertising which simply announces you are there, or *'awareness'* advertising is reserved for very large organisations who can afford the cost and seek to retain or build market share.

As an example, does your advertisement say:

*"XYZ business, where you'll find everything you need"*
*or*
*"If you open an account with XYZ by sending in the coupon within the next 14 days, we'll send you a gift worth £20".*

Neither suggestion responds to need, we'll come back to that, but there is a difference in approach. The first example tells people you are there - excellent.  The second does the same, but gets them to respond to an offer within a time period, thus providing you with the means to monitor the response to your advertisement by the number of coupons you get back.  That way, you can test which medium works best, how many people responded, and at what cost.  This measure provides a direct comparison with other marketing methods.

**A change in style to become more effective costs nothing.**

One recent campaign offered a £20 voucher to be used against the purchase of a product. Everyone who responded was given £20 off their first purchase as promised. When the first order was delivered, another voucher was provided for £35 off any further order placed before the end of that quarter.

Admittedly, the initial product cost price was in hundreds but the client had never seen a response so large before, and it certainly beat that boring old "*10% discount when you buy from us*" routine that all his competitors followed. He gave away no more than they did, but he did it in a more **inspired** way. The second voucher dramatically increased sales of his other products which could have gone to his competitors.

Response advertising is more likely to work and you get the measure of results against cost. Once secured, your loyalty scheme should keep that customer interested as long as the quality and service you provide remains good.

### HOW DO YOU WRITE AN EFFECTIVE ADVERTISEMENT

*If you are not a professional copy writer, what do you need to say to convince prospective customers that they should respond?*

There is no point in making up a story to try to attract customers - that results in an anti-climax when they take up what was an inflated offer. You have caused resentment. Tell it how it is. Avoid generalisations, slang and superlatives. Be honest but interesting. The market is there, it always will be. Your job is to exploit it, not create it.

A quotation from David Ogilvy's book on advertising gives a splendid example with the headline:

**"At 60 miles per hour, the loudest noise in the new Rolls Royce comes from the electric clock".**

It doesn't talk about the sales points of the product as you might expect, the comfort, speed, pure excellence of one of the best products in the world. What it does imply in a subtle, more effective way is the enjoyment of what is obviously a very quiet, and therefore comfortable motor car.

*Decide what's interesting to consumers about your product or service?*

Be innovative with your copy writing. At all costs, avoid the words '*also*' and '*offer*'. Either you do something or you don't and whilst anyone can **offer** anything, reputable people **provide** certain products and services. Another word that can cause resentment is '*solution*' suggesting, as it does that the consumer has a problem. There are very few instances where this word may be helpful to the message and it will not enhance your sales proposition to start with a negative. People do not like to think they have problems, as it makes them appear incompetent.

Your customers are as busy as you are. Text should be easy to understand and kept to a minimum. The use of bullet points is helpful. Be direct, succinct, and use words people understand.

The Advertising Standards Authority is quite explicit in their guidelines and rigorous in their protection. All advertising must be *"legal, decent, honest and truthful"*.

Good copy writing is an art form but if you follow certain basics from the theory books, you can do it. You start with a headline to capture attention. It can be humorous, it should be catchy and it is most important. More about headlines later. The body copy carries the sales messages appealing to need, then selling your company as the provider. Last, a call to action to tell readers what you want them to do and finally, appropriate corporate details.

*   **IDEA**: To enhance your text, see if you can find an original photograph within copyright and ask the magazine to *'lay it faintly behind the text'*, you can have an effective eye catcher for a low budget.

**THE STRUCTURE OF AN ADVERTISEMENT.**

*How do we put it all together? Let's look at the building blocks.*

You have decided what the advertisement is for, and that it appeals to a need. It should be an attractive advertisement that will catch the eye where regular readers of a magazine expect to see pages of very predictable images.

How would you describe your product to a market that had never heard of it before? Which headline would you use to capture attention? What are the USP's and where would you position them in the text to be most effective?

How could you make it *'responsive'*? If it is in colour, you could include photographs. See how the elements come together and what they are saying to the reader.

**ELEMENT 1 - THE HEADLINE:**

Headlines should start with words like *"new"*, *"now,"* *"announcing"*, *"at last"*, and preferably in *'news'* style. John Caples book *'Tested Methods'* quotes some key words to use in headlines:

**How to, How, Why, Which, Who else, Wanted, This, Advice.** He claims they are more likely to capture attention, the ultimate goal of any advertisement.

**HELP HINT**: Have you noticed what difference a few explanation marks can make?!!!! They add a sense of urgency and importance.

**CAUTION**:     Suggestive headlines are in poor taste. Those who snigger at headlines with double meanings are probably aged below the age of sixteen and are probably not your target market anyway.

Personalise your headline as much as you can with '**you**' and '**yours**'.

- "How can **you** fill your stationery cupboard without emptying **your** pockets?"
- "Where can **you** find a real choice of wheels?"  (Small van supplier).
- "Today, **you** are one of the chosen ones....."  (Who use our product)
- "Advice to **you** is free at B & B!"
  (Helps if you're in commercial insurance and your initials are good!)
- "**You'll** always do better with With!" (Name of the boss was Mr. With)

and one I devised recently for an accountant; "When did **your** accountant last call **you**?"

## ELEMENT 2 - THE BODY COPY

This is the part that sells.  Remember, be honest and do not use cliches where they can be avoided.  A maximum cliche-content of 15% is acceptable.  Phrases such as *'best deal in town'* or *' convenient location'*, *' check out...'* and *'everyday low prices'* tend to irritate customers and are seen as misleading.

Be honest: *" We have worked hard to make sure you have the greatest choice and the best value, we have convenient parking and you can have a good look round our warm, dry office furniture store, 26,000 square feet where you will be impressed with our wide range, quality and value".*

As a writing style, this text is... readable?  Did you notice, the word *'value'* was used twice? There are a few USP's in there as well.

*"Repetition sells, repetition sells, repetition sells"*

Write simply so people can understand what you mean.  Try to target people's needs, the reason why they buy.

This ad was prepared for a client and certainly attracted attention by use of the headline and the word "*FREE*". Apart from the plants, this firm provided all those services free anyway and never said so in their advertising. *They had always done it like that!*

**ELEMENT 3 - TELL THEM WHAT YOU WANT.**

It is amazing how many advertisements you will see in your trade press which do not effectively *'ask for an order'*. In marketing jargon, it is called *'a call to action'*. In the example above, prospects are encouraged to telephone for an appointment. In fact, we provide an incentive worth £15. That's innovative. How many times have you seen that tactic used to increase response and provide an opportunity to sell?

- **IDEA**: Suggest an incentive for people to respond to you. There may be a few time-wasters but you will spot them quickly. Your prospects do not receive the incentive until they visit you, the real object of the advertisement.

Advertisements can initiate the sales process by provoking people to call you for literature or you can provide other reasons for them to call, which give you the chance to sell to them.

**HELP HINT**:   If you get a response to your advertising, it should go to the top of your priority list that day. On average, 20% of all sales leads are never followed up. Amazing statistic isn't it?

- **IDEA**:   Construct a manual or computer procedure to log responses as they come in. Assign that lead to a named individual who then has the responsibility to follow it up. Check every few days to ensure all recent leads have been followed up. If you do not bother, you lose net profit.

Every advertisement should end not just with the corporate details, but with what you expect people to do.  Could you say '*thank you*' as well?  How many advertisements in your trade press say something like, *"thank you for your attention."*  Easy to gain a reputation for doing something different if no one else does?

### WRITING ADVERTISEMENTS - THE CONCLUSION

- Think about writing your advertisement as effectively as possible. Spend time on it away from the business.
- Always follow the rules.
- Appeal to people's needs.
- Be inventive and interesting.
- Log those sales leads as they come in - you **NEED** that information.

*"People respond to a need not to an advertisement."* says advertising guru Chris Lytle.

- Write for the customer, not for your profit, as one leads to the other.
- Against your annual or quarterly budget, examine the places where you feel you must advertise.  Make them as few as possible and test each continuously.
- Look at media where you could '*spot place*' and make the arrangements.
- Examine the size and position of each advertisement to maximise value to you
- Make certain you have systems in place to note response levels.
- Start a crib file
- Allocate budget to test new media
- See if the total space spend warrants handling by a media buying house.

## MARKETING METHOD NUMBER 2: DIRECT MAIL

*Direct mail is the UK's fastest growth area in promotion. How do we achieve results and what elements are needed for success?*

Amazing though it is, direct mail grew by 12% in 1995 and by a similar percentage year after year even through the recession. *'Impossible'* you may say, *'as I always throw mailshots in the bin.'* Well, so you may but obviously not everyone does, otherwise mailing promotions would not grow as rapidly as they have done. The total spend in the UK last year was £1.158Bn. That's Billion.

If you are mailing, keeping in contact with customers and prospects, communicating when the competitor down the road is not, who will do more business? It will be the company the customer remembers and you know that **repetition sells**. Active marketing of any kind can bring immediate as well as long term results and mailings are well worth a try.

Some pundits believe a mass of information, such as the ten or more pages you'll find in Readers Digest mailings, is the best way. Others feel a simple letter, leaflet and response mechanism is good enough. Both are probably correct in the right circumstances.

Again, testing and monitoring are the only proper ways to establish what will work for your business. How can you encourage people to listen to what you are saying? Remember, a direct mail letter is not the same as the sales letter you might write following a telephone call. Direct mail letters are quite different, with underlined headlines, use of boldface to emphasise various sales points, and other *'devices'* you would not find in a piece of general correspondence.

Look at the process you go through when you receive a mailshot. Before you open it, you issue a psychological challenge to the item to intrigue you, to be different. Some people let secretaries *'weed'* out mailers. Others pile them up and read them all at once at the end of a busy week and if there isn't time, they end up in the bin. But research shows that, most people do look carefully at the envelope when it arrives with other post, open it and give the item about 10 milliseconds to assess and capture interest.

So what can you do, given those circumstances?

- **IDEA**: To capture interest quickly try a 3D mailer. If you have something lumpy in it, interest and intrigue is created immediately. It might be a free pen. You'll feel it. You will definitely open it. In fact with any *'lump'*, you will try to guess what it is before you open it. Such is the inquisitive nature of most of us. When you open it, it is important for it to be immediately *worthy*.

**THE MAGNIFICENT MAILER.**

One of the most successful mailings I have undertaken for a client consisted of a simple letter, a promotional leaflet and a reply card. In the envelope, was a cork from a wine bottle.

- **IDEA**: A small card that went in the mailer, said; *"If you take up our offer, we'll give you the bottle which goes with this cork"*. When they ordered the product, we couldn't send an opened bottle through the post, so instead, we sent a £5 Threshers wine shop voucher. We enclosed a note with the voucher which read; *"We didn't want to send you a bottle as it would have arrived empty without a cork in it, and you still have the cork. So here's a voucher to get the bottle of your choice! Thank you for your order"*.

Each time I have used that idea, there has been a very high response well above average. Customers only get the voucher if they buy the product, not if they just *'send for details'*.

**TO PRINT OR NOT TO PRINT THE ENVELOPE**

You can capture attention by a message on the envelope. It might be printed with '**URGENT INFORMATION**' or '**TO BE OPENED BY ADDRESSEE ONLY**'. That will make the recipient sit up and think. Again, when the seal is broken, it must capture attention at once and be worthy of the notation on the front.

One school of thought suggests that you can interest someone faster by hinting what's inside. Any mailer is an advertisement by any other name and the process is simple. A pretty fast decision is taken very early on in the process which says - do I want this, is this product or service any use to me at all? If it is, you will want to read every word the seller can think of. If it clearly isn't of interest, it disappears pretty quickly binwards.

So by printing the front of the envelope, you hint as to what is inside and you bring the selling process forward. If you do not print the envelope, then it mustn't look anything like a mailshot. Having said that, if you just have the words **FREE GIFT INSIDE** all over it, it may well be opened faster.

As usual in marketing activity, testing is the only way to ascertain the most successful route. Try a mailing with half the envelopes printed with different messages and the other half plain, and see which works best. The other option is to attend seminars at the Direct Marketing Fair or call the British Direct Marketing Association for a course profile and make up your own mind - as opinions vary throughout the direct marketing industry. One thing is certain - mailers do work.

- **IDEA**: Send your mailer in a coloured envelope rather than a white one. They do not cost much more and might well hold enough raw interest to be opened faster. Most direct mail specialists rarely think of it. The eye is attracted by colour.

- **IDEA**: The eye responds even faster to movement. What's wrong with attracting attention using a corny pop up box if it is applicable to the market you wish to reach, or something that unfolds by itself..........? I leave that thought with you! The people that do that sort of thing are called *'cardboard engineers'*.

- **IDEA**: Try sending promotional messages via postcards. They can have a dramatic effect on response levels as they are so easy to read quickly. They have the advantage of less cost than a standard mailer pack and you might be able to send a series.

- **IDEA**: Postcards have another use. Keeping in touch with customers is critical to continued sales success. A quick hand-written card to serve as a reminder of you as a supplier could say; *"Sorry I have not been able to speak with you for a while. I will call you shortly to discuss your (product needs) for the next period shortly, kind regards"*.

One person I recall who traveled extensively used his spare time at airports to write these cards. His excuse for not being able to keep in touch was his travel commitments which sounded a reasonable excuse when in fact, the real reason was pressure of work with other clients.

**CAUTION**:  Never use *'other clients'* as a reason for not communicating frequently. It makes your customer feel unimportant.

**CAUTION**:  The Data Protection Act is an area which should be watched as you might be breaking the Law. If you prepare a mailshot using your word processor, mailmerging the names and addresses with a pre prepared letter text, you should be registered under the Act.

If you write me a letter and put my name and address at the top and after printing, it remains on your hard disk, you should be registered. I understand it is a time consuming, complicated process to become registered filling out many forms, but it is vital if you are to stay the right side of the Law and in effect, it is a necessary part of growing your business.

**HELP HINT**: Be careful how you pack your mailer. With such a short time to capture interest, it is unhelpful when the first thing they see as they open it, is the reply envelope or the back of the leaflet. All envelopes are opened from the back, so make sure the letter and clear sales message comes out first facing the prospect.

## MAILING TIPS

- *Always personalise your mailer with the recipient's name. A job title is not satisfactory. Better to put "For the attention of the person responsible for marketing" rather than "The Marketing Manager", which carries the risk that it may be considered immediately recognisable as a mailshot and the sender was too lazy to telephone to find out the correct name. A small company will not have a marketing manager as such but there will be a 'person responsible for marketing'.*

- *Try not to use labels. They give away the fact that you are selling. One new client sent his cheques by way of a label stuck on an envelope. They were mistaken for mailshots and a payment was lost. Type the address directly onto the envelope with your laser printer or use window envelopes.*

- *Always enclose a response mechanism. To be as helpful as you can to the people who want to respond to you, why not take out a Freepost address that can be obtained from your local sorting office. Don't ask a respondent to write his name and address on the reply form. Since you had to print those details on the mailer in the first place, do it again on the reply card, where a label would be quite acceptable. It will demonstrate good service and make it very fast and easy to respond.*

- *Envelopes come in many colours, but also consider shape and texture. You may find an envelope in the shape of a legal document. It might get opened faster if the recipient thinks it's a Writ.*

- *As with other forms of promotion, one mailing will not produce overwhelming results. There should always be some sort of follow up. It is said that a telephone sales follow up can double or treble the response. Another mailing to the same list with a slightly different message will have a good effect.*

- *If you repeat the mailing, don't send the same brochure twice as that is inept. The recipient thinks you have duplicated the insert when in fact, it may be a totally different mailing. People come to the wrong conclusion in 10 milliseconds.*

**WHERE CAN I FIND A LIST OF PEOPLE TO MAIL?**

What is your target market and which product will you use to approach that market? Who do you want to attract and who may become a customer? In other words, where can you find a list of people to mail who might respond to your message?

List builders abound in the UK, the USA and Europe, as do specialist list-building consultants who use worldwide data to produce a bespoke list for you directly to address your market.

All list builders can supply the information in any form: on computer disk, labels (but please don't use them unless absolutely necessary), mailmerge file, and ASCII comma delimited files. The choice of format costs no more. You can have a hard copy too and use it in-house, but there is a greater cost in labour that way.

Rented lists are rarely kept as up to date as most users expect. It costs the list builder profits to keep verifying information and so, in some cases, it may not be done as often as it should. The average invalidity content is 20%; anything over is unacceptable. List brokers will provide a credit for those not delivered.

The use of an organisation such as Dunn and Bradstreet, CCN Mosaic, or the Business Database which comes from Yellow Pages will produce a list based on current information updated frequently. There may be a minimum requirement that you buy a certain number of names.

**HELP HINT**:   I have seen a small business benefit by buying 2000 names, preparing mailings in waves of 1000, sending out 50 a week and following up every one by telephone with one person doing it all. It proved cost effective to have the mailings made up together, date as postmark of course.

- **IDEA**: Ask your list builder to give you a sample list of a dozen names from your required target area. Telephone each one a few days after probable receipt and see if they remember your mailer, what they thought and so on. Orders will be picked up this way because you were not fishing for business but testing reaction to help your mailing programme, that made the call a little unusual.

In the paragraphs above, I am really talking about cold lists or lists of prospective customers. Prospects are always the vast majority but it is worth looking close to home just in case there is a box of customers from past years that could be sorted into a list of people currently not buying from you.

- **IDEA**: The Law says you must keep your books and accounts for seven years. Do you have your sales ledger handy from three or four years ago? Those prospects would be **free** except for a minimal amount of staff time to collate lists and you have had previous dealings with them.

**HELP HINT**: If your company is about to embark on mailings or database marketing, you should start looking for a possible list from *inside* the business. Create as many opportunities as possible to collect names and addresses.

- **IDEA**: Is there a way you can gather names and addresses of prospects and thus build your own prospect database? Questionnaires are of use in this context. The value of every one is enormous because it is **free** to begin with, you own it and you can use it as often as you wish - even sell lists to other non-competing businesses if you want to.

- **IDEA**: Look around for other local non-competing companies with whom you might be able to exchange lists. Make sure you check for duplications and merge the list with yours to expand your prospect base. These additional prospects come to you free.

**CAUTION**: A word of caution. If you decide to rent a list from a list broker and you are tempted to use it more than once, having only paid for one use, resist the urge. The list renter will always find out as *'sleepers'* are put into every list automatically. Sleepers are pseudonyms that use staff addresses to know when a list has been used. It might seem very sneaky but they are after the same thing as you; a reasonable profit. It is not worth the hassle and probable Court appearance if they find out that you breached the contract. It isn't terribly fair either.

### MAILING RESULTS

Mailings, like every promotional item, must be cost-effective. The industry standard for mailing response is 1% which admittedly, seems awfully low. But in fact, if you get 1%, you achieve the average response to a cold list. You should convert 10% of the 1% . These are the figures used by some commercial agencies.

On such a low response/conversion rate, you need a very high unit/average sale to pay for the promotion and make profit. Yet, a customer gained in this way could stay with you which makes the exercise profitable. It is true that while 1% is the average response rate, it is not necessary to send out thousands to get good results and it is possible to improve depending upon the way you do it and the people you target.

Some businesses could attract more customers using invitations to special evenings, with representation from manufacturers and special offers. Breakfast Seminars have been successful for some companies when making presentations to other businesses. Once again, innovation and creativity come into play in deciding how to use mailings to attract more people to buy.

- **IDEA**: Send prospects a series of mailings, each of which contains a piece of plastic that snaps together to build a house or van which carries your name and phone number, to be used as a pen holder. By the time it is complete, they'll know who you are and what you do, as the pieces, arriving in succession with accompanying leaflets has more impact than one piece sent in isolation.

Using this theory, one client adapted the idea by sending an A4 file of good quality to all his prospects together with a few inserts. On a regular basis, he sent new inserts as new items were added to the range. The set built up into a very worthwhile catalogue of products and he enjoyed the advantage of constant communication with prospects who thought of his service first when a need arose. One other advantage in this case was the fact that because the original A4 file was of high quality, prospects were loathe to dispose of it as one would a regular mailshot.

On your own computer, using a database programme, you can capture the names and addresses to use for mailings. A modern word processing package usually provides a mail merging facility to merge a list of addresses with a standard letter. These days, that includes personalisation in salutations '*Dear Mr Rees*' and the body copy can make it a personal letter from you to the recipient even in a mailing of 5000. "*Mr. Rees, we know you will appreciate this offer....*"

If your list is too large, look in yellow pages for telephone numbers of a data preparation house who specialise in data capture. They charge around £100 - £140 per 1000 names, and can be provided on disk in your required format. Even a local secretarial business might do the work and could give you a better rate, returning the data on disk for you to load into your machine to merge with letters or invitations.

Mailsort discounts are available from Royal Mail to a maximum of 25% off the postage bill although Mailsort has a few complications. To begin with, your mailing must be in excess of 5000, and the letters have to be sorted by postcode. The sorting office will drop off hundreds of mailbags for you to use for each postcode area, to be marked and with labels to attach as they require it.

Alternatively, you could employ a mailing house and they will do all that for you but the discount might be equal to the charge. As usual, the mailing must be costed carefully but on a large enough scale, there may be savings.

Mailsort is available on letters with ordinary stamps or franked impressions. If you do not have a franking machine, the Royal Mail does. For over 500 units, they will charge an additional 3% of the postage cost; for under 500, 1p is added to the postage.

On large mailings, you might be able to have your franking done free. The local sorting office is the place to ask. They will be pleased to send a van to your office to save one of your staff struggling up the street with the load.

Another way to *'frank'* if you are printing a message on the envelope is to print the 1st or 2nd class insignia used by Royal Mail. You then pay in bulk. This is cost effective if you are printing the envelope, saving staff cost over franking with your own machine, but only on big runs.

**IDEA**: As a test, try ordering ordinary postage stamps from the Post Office and use them rather than a franked impression to see if there is any difference in response. Making the mailing look more like a *'regular communication'* can have more chance of being opened and so increase response.

Shared mailings are becoming more popular these days. Various businesses group together to send individual letters to the same prospects. This is much cheaper and less stressful but a mailing containing one of a number of sales messages rather than presenting your product on its own might mean prospects will not be reached in the best way.

The local Chamber of Commerce or networking group usually have details on participating businesses, or you could start your own.

I have said that all publicity should have a response mechanism. Coupons, order forms, or reply paid envelopes work well. BT claim that installing an 0800 number, where callers call free and you pay, can increase response by up to 3 times.

The Henley Centre published results of a survey which indicated that 80% of customers say they are more likely to call a freephone number. *"Over 75% of UK companies with freephone numbers say it has increased their business"*.

At the time of writing, installation is free on this service from BT but regulations have been relaxed and now the restriction that freephone numbers must be tied to one supplier has been removed. This means other telecommunication suppliers can provide the service.

The 0345 option, where all call charges are local wherever the caller telephones from, is another option and the use of these numbers may persuade a recipient to call you.

## MAILING FOLLOW UP

As with many features of promotion, the follow up is as important as the planning and the execution because follow up can increase response. The type and timing of the follow up is important. In telephone selling, follow up can double response.

In mailings, telephone follow up will produce at least another 2% - 3%. If the numbers of individual calls needed are too great, repeat the mailing to those who did not respond.

In press advertising, a series of at least three advertisements is needed before you can make any kind of judgement on the success of the programme. One mailing promotion could yield a large response but much depends upon the attractiveness of the offer, the design of the pieces and quality of the list.

## Summary

- While average results may seem low against costs, mailings do generate on-going business and if handled properly, will provide profits year after year.

- Decide who to target and what you will offer. Chose the list carefully so as to minimise wastage and cost.

- See if you can come up with an idea that will make your mailer 3D.

- Perhaps your business lends itself to a series of mailings that *'build'* into something the prospect will notice, or can use.

- Include some incentive, perhaps a free gift for a response. Something as simple as a pen increases response.

- Look carefully at using coloured envelopes, a really inexpensive way to be completely different at no extra cost.

- Put a time limit or closing date on the mailer to hasten response. Test, monitor and record results.

- When you make up the pack, spare a thought for the way the person who receives it will open it. In a recent study, from 72 mailing packs received in one week, only three looked as if anyone had even thought of this aspect.

- Make it easy for people to respond with a Freepost address, paid envelope, coupon or freephone number. Make the item exciting and colourful and use tints of colour if your budget will not support full colour.

If response levels reach 1%, low though that seems, you obtained the average. That made it a successful mailing campaign. Look after the customers that flow from it. They produce net profit many times over and make the original mailing more cost-effective each time they buy. Now, let us examine ways to increase response, given more budget.

**MARKETING METHOD NUMBER 3:** **AUDIO TAPES**

*You might consider preparing a cassette tape describing your product, your service or your company. Can you recall the last time you received an audio mailing?*

### *We assimilate the spoken word four times easier than the written one.*

The gravity of that statement in promotional terms is significant. The circumstances in which the recipient hears your sales message may well be significant also. We are all inherently lazy and listening to a tape on the motorway is far more appealing than being thrust a mailer, expected to study it and respond immediately in amongst lots of others.

How much easier is it to *'listen'* to a story than read a book? It could be in the car, at home, even on an evening walk or morning run with the *'walkman'*. Wherever it is, that person is likely to concentrate on what you are saying to the exclusion of other influences and that means your message will get through.

### *In fact, almost any kind of business can adapt the sales message to suit this medium and it is especially useful in areas of competition particularly against a bigger player.*

In comparison with a mailer, a tape wins hands down. In a pack, it provides the 3D lump I spoke about and so it may well be opened sooner. It will probably be the only one to arrive that day, in fact, so few people use this marketing method, it might be the only one received that month.

With traditional mailshots, many are delivered on a daily basis. Some busy managers, accumulate them for review later in the week. They usually end up binwards. Audio tapes are stored in a case or bag to listen to when next in the car. **What a difference**.

Why is audio not employed more? Perhaps it is perceived as expensive? Possibly the knowledge of how to prepare the tape is lacking? Maybe, and this is most likely, it just isn't considered. Could this be another instance of, *"We've always done it like that"?*

- **IDEA**: What could you say about your product, service or company that could lend itself to using a promotional tape? Why not jot down the elements of what you could say?

- **IDEA**: Send all your prospective customers a tape about how good your company is against their *'present supplier'*.

In relation to other forms of marketing, once your tape is made, you just roll off duplications, so costs need not be prohibitive.

Making the master tape may be more difficult unless you apply the same thinking as you would to advertising or a mailer. One way to decide what to say is to stage a role playing session with a colleague where one plays the sales person and the other the prospective customer. From that, you will elicit the sales points of your product or service. Put them in order, decide the best words which will make the point and the correct order, write some background about the company to reassure the prospect you are of good repute and reliable and, with a short introduction, you have the basic script.

It is always advisable to let someone else with knowledge of selling take a look at your draft script. An audio tape provides an opportunity to present your sales points without interruption.

Hiring a sound studio is not difficult. You will find one listed in Yellow Pages under 'Recording Services - sound' or other marketing directories. Phone for a studio rate per hour and ask about a professional voice-over artist to get an idea of costs. If it is too expensive, do it yourself - it is just like a talk you might give to the local Round Table. No 'ums' or 'errs' are allowed and any real mistakes you might make can be edited out.

You will need to edit the tape in an editing suite to produce a final version. Editing suites are hired by the hour. They can be as expensive as the original recording studio but the skilled technician is on hand to guide you. This is another area where you may be tempted to change your mind on text so keep changes to a minimum.

Tape duplications can be provided by the studio and they will advise you on where to get a box and a label printed. Later on, you might ask your customers and prospects what they think of the tape and how it might be improved. Then go back to the master tape and make some changes to refresh it.

**HELP HINT**:   You may like to think about a coupon on the label in order to make response easy, so be sure to mention it at the end of the tape. Why not make the back of that coupon a Freepost address so they do not even have to pay?

**HELP HINT**:   There is no doubt that a little library music edited on top of the voice over will help, particularly at the start where you want to attract the listener. It does cost more as it has to be hired but could be worthwhile as background music enhances the professional quality.

**HELP HINT:**   Do not forget the '*attention getter*' at the front and end with a '*call to action*'.

*Whenever you promote anything, always tell readers or listeners*
*what you want them to do.*

One benefit to remember is that with audio tape promotions, you can '*tailor*' your presentation to any particular market you are prospecting with comments directed just to those prospects. This individual approach might appear at the beginning or end of the tape with a standard presentation in the middle. This produces a highly targeted tape more likely to produce a high level of response.

If you want to be different, why not look into the costs and benefits that might come from this form of marketing. How many audio tapes can you remember being sent this year? The chances are that your competitors will not have considered this option as it is so rarely used, and that fact alone will give your company an '*edge*' in the market place.

Once having made the master tape, prospecting becomes cost effective as you will be able to order small duplicate batches to prospect with, as budget becomes available. This gives a direct measure of return against cost.

**THE AUDIO PROMOTION WITH A SPECIAL PLUS.**

An example of a successful audio promotion comes from the stationery trade where a commercial supplier used audio to bring in large account customers. This is a good example of mounting a successful promotion as all the elements are here. It began with a research programme to identify 100 companies spending over £100,000 a year on stationery.

Using actors and a professionally written script incorporating all their sales points, the company mailed an audio tape to each of the 100 prospects. Together with their tape, they mailed a Sony Walkman which meant that the prospect could listen to the tape immediately as well as receiving a business gift. The accompanying leaflets were written in such a way as to provoke them to play the tape on receipt. The mailer became a '*package*' and every one was followed up meticulously.

What would your reaction be? Would you listen to the tape on receipt if they asked you to, particularly if they provided the player? If someone took that much trouble to sell to you, would you give them a hearing? Many of them did, for in the first week, there were seven responses with requests for presentations and orders resulting from that campaign came to £1.6 million. Each '*shot*' cost £50, so for a total cost to the 100 prospects of £5000, £1.6 million turnover was the outcome. As with everything else, given good planning, execution and an adequate budget, audio tapes **do** work.

When used for a special promotion or new product launch, just think of the impact you could make with a tape. When the company grows and budgets get larger, you can add all sorts of library sounds and musical effects, to be creative.

## MARKETING METHOD NUMBER 4:                    CD MAILERS

*A technological extension to cassette tapes and electronic catalogues is the use of CD's with the capacity to carry 600 times the information of a floppy.*

At the beginning of 1996, I received my first advertising CD and since then, the medium has grown. With the ability to carry audio tracks, still pictures and video clips, it will not be long before this modern convenient medium is in much greater use for advertising.

However, far from the usual type of mailer, a CD is remarkable for the ingenuity it allows. My daughter received her first one from a night club opening nearby. They used a type of music as their USP since no other local club played it. On the CD was a very good description of the club with *'sound bites'* of laughter, chinking glasses, backed with the music. Video clips showed people enjoying themselves and obviously, they could not have achieved such a compact, powerful, visual/sound combination cost-effectively before the invention of the CD.

Recently, I needed to research a specialised list-building project for a client based on demographics and I sent for some details from a company with an appropriate product. What came back was a double CD presentation that gave me exactly what I needed, but in a unique way.

As well as raw information, it was presented interestingly with video clips showing me the sort of environment each demographic group enjoyed. There were moving shots of the house they would live in, the car they might drive and although it was information I could have done without, it helped.

But it raised an area for caution. Any use of the CD needs to be planned to a greater extent so as not to disinterest your recipient with harmless but not vital information. We are all terribly busy. It could be another area where the capability of the medium is of more interest to the marketer than the quality of the information necessary to impart.

It does look as if the marketing fraternity has found another way to impress prospects, and small businesses should be aware of what their larger competitors may be doing next. Investigate with CD producers what the real costs are.

It could cost less than a corporate video and by using all the techniques available on CD, an impressive presentation can be achieved, perhaps ahead of your larger rivals. If you find a larger competitor uses this method to your customers, see where you can add value to your production.

## MARKETING METHOD NUMBER 5:        DATABASE MARKETING

*This method could bring you instant results however small your business. Database marketing is a relatively new marketing method which is becoming increasingly popular. The technique can assist **any** size of company, particularly if you sell business-to-business. It produces the most concise targeting with the lowest wastage. If you are a small or medium-sized company with a computer, this method will earn you more business.*

### A. CUSTOMER DATABASE

Database marketing is designed to **sell more** by presenting customers or prospects with a buying opportunity, at a time when they are most likely to make a purchase.  In other words, by targeting as tightly as possible. With your computer, it will take seconds to search your customer information and create lists of those you wish to select. It is a simple step to copy them into a file of names and addresses ready to merge them with a mailshot letter making an offer specific to their need.

__CAUTION__:      There is no point at all in starting database marketing  if, at the outset, you have not established who will keep the data up-to-date and how that will be done.

### *Database marketing succeeds or fails on the accuracy of the data.*

*   __IDEA__: Why not look at your present list of customers and see how many different databases each customer could occupy.  Use the parameters of size, location, industry and product group purchased.  Add any more parameters individual to your company.

There are many ways to apply database marketing techniques. Database marketing could increase your sales levels by encouraging your present customers to buy **more** from you. This is achieved by selling them more of the product they usually buy or introducing them to different products.  The process is called '*selling up*'.  There is a high chance of success because, as present customers, they will already be aware of your good reputation.

Assume your business has 500 customers. Not **all** 500 customers buy **all** of your products. You could write to those who buy one product with a promotional incentive to buy the alternative product as well. Remember, the objective is to take out **just the target group** you *think* will provide extra sales.

You save promotional budget by targeting only the customers who may be interested in purchasing that second product range. If all the customers who **could** buy both product ranges do so, *you will sell more.*

Another database marketing idea you might apply to your customers will encourage the customers who place small orders to buy **more** from you. Maybe they share you as supplier with one of your competitors. If you could segment them from the full 500 customer base, and offer them something special to make them buy more, *you will sell more.*

Other factors to consider include the level of expenditure and product choice. These include industry type and location. Already, you have created four separate lists from your customer base, each ready to receive a proposition designed to appeal **directly to them**.

When you have made your selection and have lists available, you can decide on the best method to advance your special proposition. A mailing is the usual route but there is no reason why you could not use any other marketing method and produce good results.

The finer you target your list, the higher and more successful will be the response. It is never too early to start a database whatever the maturity of your business.

Start with a simple list comprising the company names, address, contact name, telephone number and fax number. With this information alone, which is available from your sales ledger, you have created a powerful database. You can locate customers by postcode and then sort them geographically. Add job titles to names to target the correct buyers more closely.

*Database marketing offers a purchasing opportunity to a customer with the means to buy, at the time they may be making a buying decision.*

### B. PROSPECT DATABASE

Prospective customers are another area where database marketing techniques can encourage business quickly and with reduced cost. A prospect database is always larger than your customer database. You will have less information on prospects which makes those lists more difficult to prepare.

You must adapt your prospect parameters to the requirements of your present customers. For instance, if you are successful in a particular industry, then create a list of prospects who operate in that industry. Similarly, location may be important to your business to restrict delivery costs. In this case, you could sort by postcode.

**CAUTION**:    People move from list to list. When prospects buy from you, they become customers. You must keep all lists completely up-to-date otherwise the economies of targeting are lost.

Once you have the basic details in your computer, you can start to look at how to code people on each database list. Coding is the system for making your search. You could code all the customers with a 'C' and all prospects, with a 'P'. Similarly, if you go to an exhibition and collect names and addresses, code them with an 'E' and, if it is an annual event, the year, for example PE98. Make sure that the system you choose is as simple as possible.

**HELP HINT**:   You have to be very careful with coding. If you do not plan properly at the start, you may forget why some people have a 'P' against their name or why you coded a sector in a particular way. As with most things in marketing, organise a system first and then stick to it.

**HELP HINT:**   If you are preparing lists from the same database, be sure to run a programme to identify a name that may appear on more than one list. Sometimes, it is not damaging to repeat a mailing to the same person as there will be two different types of targeted proposition. However, it is as well to be aware so that you can take appropriate action.

- **IDEA**:   Remember, some exhibition organisers allow you to buy lists of visitors after the show. The list will hold details of job title and industry type as well as name, address and company details. Consider the potential of this information for database marketing.

So far, I have looked at database marketing in general terms. Now let us go to a further stage in the coding. If your product sales depend on the size of a company, add a field to the database for *"number of employees"* or *"turnover"*. Now you can search for companies within a particular postcode area with less than 200 employees who visited your stand at the exhibition. Advice may be obtained from a database consultant who would establish how you intend to use your database and which factors you need to search on, to produce each list and get the most from it. In essence, a database is a simplified, well organised filing cabinet.

Here are some more examples to demonstrate the use of database marketing techniques. If you buy a car, your name, address and date of purchase go onto a database. A few months later you might receive a letter saying; *'It is time for your first service, absolutely free'*. In about 18 months, another letter might go out saying;' *We are previewing our new model - as a valued customer, come for a test drive before it goes on sale and we'll give you a pair of driving gloves absolutely free'*.

From time to time, lists of names are sold to other organisations, later a car-buying customer might get a letter from the AA saying, *'Your car is now 3 years old and we'll give you 10% off AA full cover if you apply within the next 7 days.'* This is a good example of networking or teaming your database up with another business.

- **IDEA**: There may be companies near you who have databases that could be of use to you - and yours, to them. Does your company accept credit card payments? If your business agrees to use a credit card company to take your customer's payments, some will lend you their list of card holders in your district from which you can construct a list to mail. If you are a growing business, which non-competing organisation could you network with to share databases? It only takes one telephone call to make the suggestion.

As another example, let us say you sold photocopiers and accessories and owned a list of companies who have one. That enables you to sell other products a photocopier owner needs to a highly targeted list. You could sell them copier paper, of course. But what else can you sell people who have a copier? Cartridges of toner, special pads to keep a note of how many copies each department uses, pens to write the information with and so on. Doubtless you can devise similar product promotion opportunities for your business. Compile the list of names of all the people who bought the copier paper and drop them a note about the special terms on your recycled cartridges, for one month only. This is the essence of selling up using a database.

Database marketing is a powerful weapon in the marketing tool box and results will be high if you have selected your list correctly. The following example demonstrates this. It also provides a solution to the problem of recovering lapsed customers.

One client had all his customers and prospects on a computer database. To assess the extent of possible lost sales, I suggested that a search be made, to discover how many customers had not made a purchase during the previous three months and what those customers had purchased at the same time, the previous year.

It transpired that out of 2200 customers on the database, 600 had not made a recent purchase. During the same period of the previous year, those 600 customers accounted for turnover worth £90,000. If that business failed to contact those customers with some form of offer to attract them back, £90k was the potential loss of turnover to that business.

Having that information meant that sales actions could be constructed to retrieve lapsed customers who are easily identifiable from computer reports and are a quick source of extra sales and profits, if not the fastest. The database programme in the example above should have been run every month, some might argue every week to keep the numbers of customers identified in more manageable numbers for promotional action.

By implementing this procedure, you may be able to keep the majority of customers because you are in full possession of the information regarding who has not purchased recently and might be lost to your business. You can take action quickly to identify them and retrieve the account. Database marketing techniques can be applied to different categories of customers and prospects, within your business and outside it.

- **IDEA**:   Get your accounts department to conduct the same exercise on your records and see what your loss might be if you do not act quickly to retrieve those who have lapsed. Set up systems to conduct the same exercise on a monthly basis.

Another interesting example of database marketing was reported by the BBC. The Conservative Party, concerned about voters in marginal constituencies employed database marketing techniques in their attempt to win the 1997 election.  Twenty thousand key prospects were identified in a series of marginal constituencies using demographic criteria which suggested they were marginal voters and each received a series of mailings in an attempt to persuade them to the cause. Letters signed by Prime Minister, John Major and received locally, indicated the selection of those who had recently made share purchases as targets for the campaign in my area.

- **IDEA**: A manufacturer might be interested in paying for a special mailing to your database, carrying your name as the local supplier of their product.  This could be a free promotion for you and it could save a large slice of your promotional budget whilst still giving you exposure to regular and prospective customers.  Your database has targeted consumer names, a manufacturer does not.  As with everything else, if it has the desired effect, the manufacturer can then be encouraged into more grandiose schemes.

Database marketing can become complicated depending on how far you want to take it.  As a tried and tested means to sell more, it is the modern method and most large commercial organisations are either doing it, or looking closely at the possibilities.  As always, the measure is cost against benefit and the first thing you need is to create a good database and appoint a qualified person who can keep it current and make the most use of it.

### SUMMARY

- There is no doubt that database marketing saves considerable waste of promotional budget by targeting more directly.

- Saving budget, selling more at the right price to those who can buy at that time will increase net profit.

- Can you apply the principles to your business?

- Which member of your staff could best be employed to keep the database updated?

*You may already have the information.  Using it properly, more effectively costs nothing*

## MARKETING METHOD NUMBER 6:      TELEPHONE  SELLING

*This is a method that many people do not feel suits them but in fact, anyone with determination and understanding of the basics can achieve a result from selling on the telephone. This chapter tells you how to start. If you are experienced, then rediscover the basics.*

### ARE YOU GETTING THE MOST FROM YOUR TELEPHONE?

We handle telephones constantly but most of us could get so much more from it by looking carefully at the potential it holds.

Many people feel inhibited when using the telephone to sell.  But in business, the telephone can produce more for you than any other form of promotion, with it's ease of use and instantaneous results. Even a novice can increase sales from every call that comes in regardless of the intention of the caller, and as an instant door opener, it is unbeatable.  Rather than just *'dealing'* with the call and getting on to the next thing, why not examine how each call could be used to capture more business?

### BASIC TECHNIQUE

Anyone can do it. Using the telephone to sell or present your company starts with your personality. People buy from people. Selling is largely a matter of conversing to identify a need. You do not have to be hard, forceful, or unpleasant, be professional.  By following a few ground rules, using the knowledge of your product, understanding your customers needs and your overall approach could be enough to get you some important sales appointments or to make some sales.

Before you start any promotional activity, you need to think about the products to promote and the most likely people to produce sales for you.  As a small business, you have the advantage of speed of reaction to requirements and personal service as sales points already.

Decide the sales points in order, using the correct words.  Type them up and stick them on the office wall - you just never know when you may need instant help. If you think this way, every time the telephone rings, you will use that list.

- **IDEA**:  If you are new to using the telephone, when you encounter a problem, write it down and decide what you should have done.

You will find that these problems are repeated.  This becomes a means of self-training and learning how to improve.

Calls come in to all your staff all day long and everyone needs to be aware of the opportunities. You may see your telephone as a communication tool, a means of taking orders, confirming arrangements, settling problems and of course it is. But if you apply **marketing** aspects, might you get more from it? The basic principles of marketing dictate that you should *'sell up'* to customers and *'convert'* prospects.

- **IDEA**: The next time the phone rings, during the conversation, try to sell something to that person regardless of their reason for calling.

## SELLING UP

When a call comes in from a customer wishing to place an order, you should look at the conversation for any opportunity to carefully sell the caller more than he wanted. Apart from suggesting a higher discount for buying a greater quantity, there are two ways to do that. One is to sell him more from your range of products, another is to convince him to take a higher margin line.

You have to develop the skill to think as you talk. Most of us are pretty good at doing one or the other, doing both takes practice. Listen to what is being said. Is the customer seeking advice? Does he want information on which to base a decision? Is he quite clear in what he wants or open to suggestions? Are there associated products connected with those being ordered?

As most businesses have one, let's use the photocopier example again. If a customer calls with an order for copier paper, it is a fair guess he has a copier. What else could you sell him? Well first, more copier paper than he requested by offering a special price or promotion.

> *"You may not realise Mr Smith, we have a special offer on at the moment. If you order one hundred reams instead of fifty, I can give you an additional 5%. You might like to take advantage of that?"*

> *Or*

> *"Mr Smith, if you are not too sure which chair you need, could I suggest the Regency. It is within EC regulations, very comfortable and I have a choice of three colours in stock at the moment. What is your colour scheme?"*

The Regency is the most expensive line. This seller takes the customer's mind off the need for a chair and into the colour he prefers so he is thinking *"what colour do I want?"*, not *"shall I buy a chair?"*

### INCOMING CALLS - ANY POTENTIAL THERE?

As your experience grows, you will see opportunities in every call even when a customer phones to complain. In fact, there are those who feel that is one of the best times to sell hard.

When a customer has a complaint, you have to deal with it sympathetically and appease them. If you do that properly, you have a superb opportunity to sell. Give the customer space to vent their anger without interruption. They will soon '*burn out*', you can solve the problem and re-establish the relationship. Start asking questions about the products under complaint, or explain the rest of the range you have available. I have known cases where big orders have been taken from a conversation which started as a dispute. It is all about thinking ahead, putting yourself in their position and being professional.

### WHO'S GOING TO DO IT?

You could employ a tele-marketing company if you do not think you have the requisite skills in house. As usual, the range of tele-marketing services varies. There may be a sizeable minimum fee which buys you a certain number of calls that are made following preparation of a script. A tele-sales company in Hertfordshire has a setup cost of just £75 and charges 95p a call per connected recipient with no minimum. It does pay to '*shop around.*'

There are a number of other tele-marketing companies and these can be found in a copy of the Marketing Handbook. They work in similar ways. The writing of the sales story into a script is paramount. Decide the list of prospects you wish to call, the sales points to be presented, the end result you require. The calls are made and the results are yours immediately.

Working to a script, there will be times when the tele-sales person does not know the answer to a question. When this happens, a call back is promised within one hour, from someone at the client's firm. This way, service to the customer is maintained.

### WHAT HELP IS THERE?

If you do not have budget to spare for a tele-sales firm, try it yourself. If you are really interested, attend a course run by the British Direct Marketing Association or another training organisation which your local Chamber of Commerce should be able to suggest. Business Link in your area are likely to run courses as well. Telephone sales is like everything else. Once you have some skill, you'll wonder why you didn't do it earlier.

- **IDEA**: One thing you should learn on a tele-sales course is how to break through the '*guard dog*' secretary who will not let you through to speak to her Boss. Before you give up and write a series of letters instead, try phoning at 8.00 am. It is amazing how many executives start work before the "*guard dog*" arrives. A daytime fax is another good way past looking like a bona-fide business communication. Send it before 9.00am

## THE AIMS

If you have decided to try, set your objective. Telephone selling is designed to break new ground, persuade prospects to give up a present supplier and use your company. Appreciate the risk for the prospect in doing that when they know nothing about you. There should be a number of reasons, not only better prices.

Do not set out with the idea you can make a few calls and eliminate the competition. Set the sights lower at first. Seek a trial order, an attempt to *"prove your service"*. If your prospect buys different product ranges, try to supply just one. Service it well, build the relationship and then go for more by selling up.

Do not be put off if a trial order is not given on the first call. In that event, ask for a commitment. *"Next time you need an (product), will you use us?"* That gives you something to remind the prospect he said the next time you call.

## COLD SELLING ON THE TELEPHONE.

Once again, anyone can do it. Hard selling is forcefully persuading someone to take your product by whatever means. Small businesses hardly ever indulge in this. We have said that people buy from people and your personality and product knowledge are by far the most important factors. Large measures of brandy or adrenalin are not necessary, it can be very rewarding when each call you make turns out well.

There are basic techniques which can help. In order to make a product appeal to a potential buyer, there are things the seller needs to know to establish if there is a need for the product and the best way to present it. Remember, that buyer has left a task to answer the call. It is very important that the experience turns out to be good use of time.

Little success will come from the seller making a personal introduction, then reeling off a list of sales points. Any information gained can be used to interest a buyer. So first, buyer and seller must converse. All *'conversations'* ask questions. If I ask you what you had for breakfast, you will tell me. We are conversing. If I wait for you to tell me, I may never find out.

## OPEN ENDED QUESTIONS

In telephone selling, there are two types of questions; 'open-ended' questions start with key words such as *"Who", "What", "When", "How", "Why"* and *"Which"*. Construct some sentences starting with these words and you will see they cannot be answered by *'yes'* or *'no'*. They prolong conversations and lead to an opportunity to sell.

- **<u>IDEA</u>**: Write down the sort of questions you need answered to give you information that could lead to closing a sale of your products? What do you need to know?

***Open ended questions are the key to sustaining and controlling a sales conversation***

*Some examples:*

*How many staff do you have?*
Gives an indication of the size of the company and the level of a trial order.

*"What size is your average order?"*
Can lead on to telling you if they are on a contract, if they use a local competitor, if they buy via mail order and so on.

*"What other office products do you use?"*
Gives an idea of the range of your products this person might need.

*"How long have you been working at XYZ Mr Smith?"*
Leads to whether or not he has buying responsibility, prospects like to talk about themselves.

*"What sort of chairs do you normally purchase?"*
This starts talking about chairs, not about whether to use you as a supplier.

*"Where do you usually buy them?"*

*"How many do you buy?"*

*"How often do you buy them?"*

*"What price do you expect to pay?"*

*"Do you prefer chairs with detachable arms?"*

*"Does all your office furniture conform to EC directives?"*

Questions on their information technology tell you if there is scope for IT related sales but also, if they would be amenable to an electronic catalogue or ordering on line. Every question provides valuable information on the prospect's buying habits giving you the maximum chance to sell products from your range at the price he is used to when the right time comes.

## CLOSED QUESTIONS

Questions answerable by *'yes'* and *'no'* are called 'closed' questions and sometimes, you need them, for instance, to close the sale, such as *" Can I take your order?"* or *"Next time you need a supplier, will you use us?"* They have a use in establishing a position so you can be sure you are on the right track: *"Do you use these products Mr Rees?"* or *"Are you the right person to talk to about this Mr Rees?"*

## THE STRUCTURE OF A COLD SALES CALL

Cold telephone selling is a marketing method used to make sales but it can be used to arrange visits which provide an opportunity to secure larger accounts. The best way to convince a business they should be buying from you is face-to-face. There is no substitute for assessing reaction in person, presenting your case, watching your adversary and answering objections. A meeting gives the opportunity to close the sale, secure the order, even sign the contract.

Most business people are far too busy to see *'a sales person'* and so your first task is to use the telephone to convince the prospect that he should invest the time to talk to you face-to-face. The other primary purpose of telephone selling is to achieve sales.

In some cases, it may be helpful to call to find the name of the appropriate buyer. Then when you call to sell, you can ask for the correct person by name which suggests you already have a relationship. That way, you will increase the chances of being put through.

The call should start with who you are. It is a sign of professionalism to use your surname.

*"Good morning, Andy Thomas here from XYZ Stationers."*

If somebody begins a sales conversation without using their surname, you know at once that they are badly trained.

## BE CONFIDENT, PROFESSIONAL AND SOUND EFFICIENT.

The next portion is critical and should be a statement to capture attention, much as a headline does in an advertisement. It needs to be informative, intriguing and capture the prospect's interest. Your prospect probably realises you are selling and so this statement becomes very important to the continuance of the call. Here's an example of how quickly you can lose someone's attention:

*"Good Morning Mr Rees, My name is Darren from Copiers Unlimited, just a courtesy call to see if you have any office machine requirements at the moment?"*

Answer, No, call ended.  A total waste of time.  If you or your staff ever use the phrase *'courtesy call'* such meaningless verbiage demonstrates a lack of training and innovation. Worse, it cannot capture attention.

Having established who you are, holding the buyer's attention, then begin the conversation with your first question.

> *"Good morning Mr Phillips. My name is Andy Thomas from XYZ Stationers. We are planning to invite some local business people to our new showroom shortly for a seminar on the effects of recent EC directives.* ***Do you know how they could affect you?"***

You should get a *'no'* to this question. Mr Phillips probably does not have much time to study EC directives which do not relate to his industry. Apart from when you ask for the order, it's one of the few times in the conversation you want a *'yes' or a 'no'*.  Usually *'yes'* and *'no'* tend to *complete* a conversation rather than prolong it.

During a recent telephone sales course, a delegate could not understand why he was having so much difficulty getting the conversation going until I pointed out, all his questions were *'closed'* generating one-word responses.

You will understand that in our example, the sales person is selling office furniture. The next stage is to create a conversation by asking a series of relevant questions which leads to gathering information and creating a relationship. Such questions might be, **what** sort of furniture have you got, **how** long have you had it, are you the person who orders new desks, does your office furniture conform to the EC directives, **what** style do you prefer, **when** did you last change it, **who** did you go to, **what** plans are there for refurbishment?  You are seeking information to help you present sales points when the time comes.

**HELP HINT**:  Do not be afraid to ask *"why?"*  If you receive a 'negative' statement such as: *"We would never use your company"*, answer by asking; *"Why is that Mr Rees?"*  The prospect will respect you for asking and give you an opportunity to reply positively.

You need to tailor your questions to the area of the market into which you wish to sell, to look for a prospect's need, to probe the weaknesses which your product could fulfil and offer an opportunity for you to present your sales points. Ask the prospect **which** products he buys, **when**, **who** from, **how** much, **what's** the service like?

If a customer has large buying needs, there might be a contract in place for a period of time. Ask all about the contract, how big is it, how many products are on the contract list, where is the present service falling down, what service does he require and most important, when is the renewal date?

## HOW TO DEAL WITH COMPETITORS

When you learn news of a competitor, far from being a negative, this is a conversion opportunity. Ask who it is, how good are they, what products are they supplying, how often do they deliver? When you have all the good points and with the prospect secure in the knowledge that you can not refute that he is well served, ask some more pertinent questions such as;

*"Have they ever let you down, when, over what?"* Ask, *"What improvement would you welcome?"* Let's face it, we all fail in some respect sometimes. Armed with this information, use it. The prospect might tell you, *"They are very good but often, there's something left off the order and we either have to wait for it or the driver goes back for it"*. Do not critisise that competitor, but tell the prospect how well your quality assurance people work. Then time for some more general chat, hold the complaint in reserve until the time is right to SELL.

Talking about your competitors provides information about them you may not have known and it provides a sales opportunity as well. Most prospects will react reasonably when you have them talking about their present suppliers. Never run competitors down. That is unprofessional and engenders resentment. Tell the prospect how good **you** are, not how dreadful they are.

A very good question to ask is, *"Are you 100% satisfied with the service you are getting?"* Notice, that starts with '*Are you*' so he has to say *yes* or *no*. If he says *yes*, is he being truthful? Possibly not as after a time, there is always something that niggles about a present supplier. They may be slightly late or the order is not complete. Perhaps the usual contact has passed your account to a junior. Question, how is service lacking? Note his comments and bring them back as sales points when it is time for you to sell as I will show.

> *"I find that my orders are sometimes short. They do try but the new girl on the switchboard is not very efficient, she puts me through to the wrong department."*

When the time comes for you to sell, you might say;

> *"I understand about short deliveries Mr Rees, it is frustrating isn't it. Happily at XYZ we don't have that problem as we employ three quality control people to check every order. I should say that you can by-pass the switchboard! We use order hot lines and your company is allocated to one of our permanent advisors - you can always deal with the same person if you wish."*

You can see from this example that the technique is to get as much information from the prospect as you can and use it back at him as selling points later. If you find out what upsets him, you can decide which sales points will answer that. Effectively, he will sell himself with you guiding the questions down the desired route.

Sometimes, it takes more than one telephone conversation to get to this point which is why you need to take notes as you speak, and at the end of the call. Most importantly, make a diary entry for the date to call back together with what to say then.

Needless to say, if you can get your prospect to visit your premises to show him around, you could secure some business if all the other factors such as range, price and quality are in place. Here is a variation of the conversation above that leads to a visit.

> *"You may know that we have three people in our quality control section and their job is to check each order to make sure it is complete. So far this year, we have only had one incident when a courier mislaid a box. When would you like to visit us and see how well that department works?"*

After most sales conversations, it is best to write a letter so that a prospect has something to keep in his file against future need, as well as a reminder of the points you have made. You may send him a corporate brochure but the letter needs to repeat the sales points you made in your conversation.

## BUYING SIGNALS

During the conversation, the prospect will make buying signals, phrases that tell you it *'could'* be time to close the sale. They are very easy to miss as they come in so many different forms. Examples would be phrases such as; *"I must say, that sounds better than the chair I have, how much is it?"*

When the prospect asks a question, you know you have interest. Be truthful with the answer and ask another question on the same subject to keep it going.

Other buying signals may be; *"What colours are there?"* or *"What's the delivery time?"* They wouldn't ask if they were not interested.

## SALES POINTS

When the opportunity to sell arises, what will you say? Which words will present the sales points correctly and in what order should they be presented? You cannot do that off the top of your head, even if you have been selling for 20 years.

*   **IDEA**: Take a minute to write down the sales points which fit your product and your company. Choose the correct words to describe each point, put them in the correct order, and pin a copy above the telephone. Each time you come to sell, read them again, even though you are positive you know them. Your presentation will be well planned and faultless every time. Not many sales people can do that.

Many people trust their memory or claim that; *"as they have been doing it for so long anyway, there's nothing they can improve on"*.

## ASKING FOR THE ORDER OR 'CLOSING'

The moment of truth. The call to action. I want your business.

The most common mistake made by a tele-sales person is failing to ask for the order and close the sale. If you cannot get an order, you **can** get a commitment. *"Next time you need (my product), will you use us?"* The next question would then be; *"When will that be?"* and that puts you right back in the sales conversation again. At worst, you have a firm date to call back and you can remind the prospect of what was promised.

There are many words and phrases you can use to close the sale. They come in the form of closed questions such as, how many would you like, which address would we be delivering to, which model do you prefer? It is rare to ask; *"Can I have your order?"* as the prospect might say no, but this phrase is a firm and precise no nonsense approach. *"Is there a requirement coming up soon that could give us the opportunity to prove our service to you?"* might be less direct or; *"Can my company supply your next requirement?"* Choose the style to fit the situation. If he says no, ask why.

If you want to visit the prospect, ask. *"I am in your area next Wednesday, what time are you free?"* By considering the time he might see you, he may miss the fact that he does not want to see you at all.

## OBJECTIONS

Objections come in different forms. During any sales conversation, you must be ready for difficult moments when the prospect makes an objection to the sales points you are putting forward.

The rule is to turn an objection into a positive point, much like a politician avoids answering a question without changing the subject. In telephone selling, you **do** need to answer the question by countering with benefits and ending with a question to continue the conversation. Here are some common objections which might stop you in your tracks if you are unprepared with suggestions of how to counter them;

**Prospect**: *"Your prices are too high."*

**Tele-sales person**: *"The price reflects the very high quality of this product. It has x, x, x, and x. How much budget will we be working with as I may well be able to find a product of suitable quality?" (x = a benefit)*

**Prospect**: *"You can't deliver fast enough."*

**Tele-sales person**: *"Many of our customers use us against competitive companies because of our fast deliveries. They are very impressed with our scheduling. I will talk to the Distribution Manager when we have finished this conversation: When do you need delivery?"*

**Prospect**: *"I am very happy with my present suppliers."*

**Tele-sales person**: *"Well, I would not want to interrupt a satisfactory arrangement, but we do have a bigger product range than them. Let me ask you, are you 100% satisfied with the service you get, have they ever let you down?"*

**Prospect**: *"Well send me the details..."*

This is the way the prospect will get rid of you - or try to. Many tele-sales people give up at this point because the prospect is indicating he has had enough. There are ways to get round this objection, the direct route!

**Tele-sale person**: *"Of course, when can I drop them in to you? Will three o'clock suit you?"*

The more traditional method:

**Tele-sales person**: *"Of course, what exactly are you interested in...?"*

That way, you can carry on as you have used an open ended question which the prospect has to answer. This allows you to explain the feature he mentioned and steer the conversation back to your objective.

Have you noticed how objections look like buying signals? Look at how the tele-sales person always asks another open ended question to continue the conversation.

When objections such as these appear during conversations, it takes **planning** to produce a good answer to an objection and **experience** to turn it into a sales point. Invariably, you can decide beforehand what a prospect might object to and think how to counter it. As you go through a tele-sales programme, prospects will come up with objections you may not have considered, so write them down and decide how to counter them next time they arise.

- **IDEA** Role play a sales conversation with a colleague. Make as many objections to your sales points as you can think of and decide which product benefit will best counter them.

- **<u>IDEA</u>**: If you have not heard of ***the magic pause***, this technique is well worth a try. Have a conversation with someone and stop talking at the end of a sentence. Do not say another word. Pause....

The other person will speak first. It is difficult to know why but it is a technique taught in most telephone sales courses as it helps gain time to think.

### FOLLOW UP

*You will stand out from the rest.*

Never expect a prospect to call you back, however many times they say they will. In short, they won't - ever. You have to do it - always. The tele-sales person who calls back when they say they will is the one who will get the order. It might take a couple of months, it could take a year and in practice, most give up and move on to other prospects. But in the end, prospects will get to know you and if you have performed professionally, you will get your chance. Your initial follow up will be the sales letter. Your subsequent follow up will be another call. Use the diary. You will never remember unless you make a diary entry the minute the call has ended. That next call **could** be the one to bring in the business. If you forget it, **all** the work is lost.

This process does work. Once, I obtained business from a prospect I had been talking to for well over two years and they became regular clients after I proved my service.

- **<u>IDEA</u>:** The best way to keep track of a tele-sales campaign is by maintaining a manual or computer record card and creating a prospect database. Make a concise account of each conversation, areas of prospect interest, objections, **then note what to say on the next call**.

- **<u>IDEA</u>**: This is the secret to success and one most people never think of. Will you be able to remember how to approach the prospect two months later without repeating yourself? If you can refer to concise notes, you will go to the heart of any negatives with a positive approach to close the sale.

**<u>HELP HINT</u>**: If you do have to call over an extended period, write letters after each call. They will all go into your file making it look efficient and professional, giving you an edge with that prospect company over competitors by getting the targeted sales points on paper.

**<u>HELP HINT</u>**: Identify the market. You can identify good prospects by the profile of the customers you serve at the moment. Which sector of the market might produce your best chance for profits? With which industry are you doing well at present? It is important to identify the market which works where your products are successful and to concentrate there.

Remember lapsed customers, the fastest source of new sales. Call and find out if you have let them down in any way? Show concern and ask for another chance to prove your service.

Make a start and try telephone selling. Like everything else, it takes time to become proficient but if you are running a business, you have too much experience to be deterred with the first few calls not going well. On every call, you learn something new.

## SALES TEAMS

Creation of a cold selling telephone team can lead to a number of other benefits. If you decide to attack your local commercial market place with a tele-sales cold canvassing programme, it will lead to more accounts being opened and a better motivated sales force. Business life becomes more interesting and the competitor who continues to be passive in this area is disadvantaged.

It is usual to train tele-sales staff on an external course although some firms supply outside trainers who will come to you and put your staff through an intensive period of familiarisation and improvement.

Part of the planning is organising territory, establishing market criteria such as the size and type of company who will buy your product, the number of calls that represents a reasonable workload and details of any commission scheme you will adopt.

Once you have your people in place, how will you organise? One of the things a trained tele-sales person will do is **qualify** all new accounts against your pre-determined criteria. This uses categories from: *'not much good'*, to *'very hot prospect'* and shades in between. Each category needs a different approach.

Very hot prospects or potentially very large accounts will need a visit. Will that be by your representative or you? If it's the former, then every minute he or she spends doing anything other than selling for you is a waste of your time and money.

Setting up two or three sales teams provides another element - internal competition and all sales people believe they are the best all the time.

It is common in some industries to call order takers *'telephone sellers'*. Working with a sales team, a good order taker will increase the team result by selling up to everyone who calls in to place an order.

One really good team in a client's sales department comprised four people. There were two cold tele-sales canvassers, one order taker and a representative.

This team worked well together. They were on a shared bonus and each covered for the other, got each other out of difficulty, and motivated and trained each other. They did very well for their employer.

This team arrangement suits highly motivated staff and brings in handsome rewards for you. You might decide to expand by creating a team to attack a particular segment, key market or a difficult competitor. Firms who operate in this way often employ Key Account Executives to open new, high value accounts and keep them going. In terms of cost, this is the big league but that said, high returns follow over a long period from such an investment, even when sales people may well have moved on to another challenge.

- **IDEA**: Why not provide a few trips to Europe for the winning section as competitive teamwork is known to work well for commission based staff? Obviously, when they are successful, those new accounts could be with you for many years if you treat the new customers properly.

In the next section on sales letters, we cover the points you need to take into account when writing a sales letter following up on a telephone sales call.

**THE NUMBERS GAME.**

If you have heard of the numbers game, you will already know that the more calls you make, the more business you'll get. It is the way of working out how many telephone calls it takes to get an appointment, then the number of appointments it takes to get the business.

By altering the '*mix*' and including sales letters and newsletters, these additional contacts with your prospect cut down the number of telephone calls needed to make the sale. Again, it's all about testing. Sales letters are important to reinforce what has been said and the subsequent action you intend to take. It is part of the process of getting to know the customer and forming a relationship.

- **IDEA**: Enclose a free pen in your sales letter. It is a useful way to leave your telephone number and gives you an '*edge*' in the prospect's mind.

**FINAL TELEPHONE SALES TIPS AND SUMMARY:**

- **Your diary and record card are the key**. Those who call back as promised, knowing what to say, obtain the business.

- Follow up every call with a letter. Follow up every letter with a call.

- Aim for a trial order, not the whole account, not yet.....

- Counter objections with a positive benefit.

- Think positive. They have to buy from someone.

- Never send a sales letter without planning and constructing the approach as it can do more harm than good.

- Always call first to find out the name of your prospect buyer so you talk to the right person with buying responsibility and qualify the potential.

- Establish a need before you start heavy selling otherwise your prospect will lose interest.

- Use each conversation to form and continue a relationship with the prospect, person to person.

- Always note what you will say the next time you call.

- Note objections you countered and the best way to continue the call to reach a conclusion. In forming a relationship, this is very helpful.

- Anyone can do it.

## MARKETING METHOD NUMBER 7: THE 'COLD' SALES LETTER

*In this section, we look at the 'cold' sales letter, the communication that should lead to the next stage in the sales process. Sales letters following a telephone call are covered later in this chapter.*

Almost all small businesses fall into a common trap when writing cold sales letters. The attitude is there is no time to plan, sales are low and **something** needs to be done quickly. The result is an unplanned, illogical letter and because you have not thought carefully about it, the letter carries little chance of success.

A letter to the prospect company that explains in the first paragraph what **you** do and who **you** are, is the way most people start because they think they should be selling. In fact, this is **not** the best way to persuade a prospect to buy from you for the first time because you have not given a reason why they should. All selling depends upon the buyer having a need. If there is no **need**, there will be no purchase, because in commercial selling, impulse purchases are difficult to achieve.

Here is an example from a letter that I received while writing this section. Almost every sales letter from a small business is constructed like it.

*Quest Consultants Ltd.*
*The Courtyard*
*Hertford, Herts*
*SG14 1EQ.*

*Dear Sir,*

*We are a multi-franchised car management organisation whose functions are to source, buy, and dispose of motor vehicles on behalf of our clients, these include cars, car derived vans and panel vans..................*

**CAUTION**:     Beginning a letter with the salutation *"Dear Sir"* is **very** risky. What if the MD is a woman? With one action, you may have lost any chance with that company as the result of making one, classic error. Years ago, *"Dear Sirs"* was acceptable. Today, equality demands that you check or cover yourself with *'Dear Sir or Madam'*.

**HELP HINT**: In the example, notice the description, *'car derived vans'*, a technical term, probably well understood in that business but not necessarily by the rest of us. A lack of understanding causes an immediate lack of interest.

In any growing business where time is at a premium, you might not take the necessary time to telephone the prospect first. But there are things you need to know. What potential do they hold for you, who is the person responsible, how many staff are there? Receptionists are quite happy to give you any information if you take the trouble to telephone or call in.

The principle of correct targeting is well established in these pages. It is imperative to get the name of the person responsible and the consequences of not doing so are obvious. As well as dealing directly with the person who makes the buying decision for that prospect company, you know who to call when you follow up.

**HELP HINT:** Unless you are conducting a blanket mailing, telephone first to find the right name, the correct spelling, job title and to *'qualify'* the prospect to see if there is potential for them to buy from you. If not, go on to the next prospect aware that you saved marketing budget and net profit by not selling to the wrong person without the responsibility, or the need to buy

.

Let us look at the first paragraph of the example letter again.

> *"**We** are a multi-franchised car management organisation whose functions are to source, buy, and dispose of motor vehicles on behalf of **our** clients, these include cars, car derived vans and panel vans."*

In the sample letter, the seller uses *"We"* or *"Our"* twice and *"you"* or *"yours"* not at all. The letter comes across as one written for the writer, not for his potential customer and every sales letter written by non-professional sales or marketing people carries the same errors.

As with advertising, mailings and any other form of promotion, you must capture attention in the opening sentence. Don't start your letter talking about **you**, what **you** do and how good **you** are. It may be natural selling behavior but **it is not** the best way. How many people do you meet for the first time who say to you, *"Hello, my name is Tim, I'm absolutely terrific at everything"*? What would you think of them if they did? So why do it in a sales letter?

People buy when they have a need. What need can you create that will capture attention? Talking about **your** company or **your** activity will not do. In our example, would it have been better to say *"Do you have a company car that you need to sell quickly?"* That addresses them with a need, and by posing a question, you ask the prospect to think of an answer.

Another way might be *"Are your vehicle costs too high?"* That might make people think about what they do cost as we all want to cut costs if possible.

- **IDEA**: Take an example of a sales letter you have written recently. Count how many times in the first paragraph you refer to your prospect and how many times you refer to you. How many times have you used the word *"you"* or *"yours"* as you should, and how many *"we"* or *"ours"*?

- **IDEA**: Re-write your sales letter using the principles above. Send a sample number of your old text and the same number of rewritten ones and note any difference in response when you telephone to follow up.

Having prepared a first sentence that will capture attention, you must **hold** that attention in the first paragraph, to expand the need, not present **yourselves** as the solution. Not yet.

In our example, the letter went on to say:

> *"If you operate one vehicle or a fleet, regardless of the type of business, **we** will demonstrate the same level of care and consideration, in fact **our** whole system is geared to ensure customer satisfaction, for **we** believe the key to success is customer retention."*

In the second paragraph, there are three references to **our** or **we** and one to **you**. The paragraph is selling too early, before a need has materialised, and the phrasing of the last line suggests this company is more interested in their profit than providing a satisfactory service to the prospect. The letter continued for five paragraphs in the same style and finished with a creditable call to action that said:

> *"Contact **us** and arrange a meeting to discuss **your** next vehicle acquisition, and join **our** growing client base, that use and enjoy **our** excellent service."*

This paragraph contains three references to the seller and one to the buyer. Apart from some poor layout, at least the end asks the prospect to act, which is good. However, why ask to *'contact us'*? Would it be more personal to say, *'contact me'* or perhaps, *'please telephone me?'* After all *'we'* did not sign the letter, *'I'* did. This letter is a demonstration of why someone else should read it before it is sent.

You will see that constructing a letter which will have the maximum chance of success with your prospect demands a little more thought.

### LETTERS TO FOLLOW UP A TELEPHONE SALES CALL

*Sales letters that follow up a telephone call, a visit or an appointment are different from 'cold' sales letters, as you have some knowledge of the prospect's needs.*

There is a distinction between a '*sales letter*' and a '*mail shot*'. It is accepted that both are '*selling*' but the layout of a mailshot follows guidelines more akin to advertising while a sales letter is a letter from me to you on my headed paper.

There will be many times in the sales process when a well timed sales letter can make the difference between helping you towards the close, and such a letter, aimed to arrive following a contact with the prospect, can be most important. Like everything else, some people enjoy letter writing, others abhor it. But if there is a creative writer amongst your sales team, they will help by confirming tele-sales conversations, re-stating sales points and generally keeping in touch with your prospects.

The most successful person is one who combines tele-sales skills with creative writing and you will find them making a call, writing a letter, making a call, writing a letter.

Some sales people find this irritating, difficult and a dreadful time taker. Sadly, their letters reflect this attitude and there are even some who are so bored by the whole enterprise, they send standard letters to everybody. This misses the opportunity to be individual, and target the presentation to the needs of that individual prospect. A standard letter presents poor representation of your sales points, and is completely un-targeted. It cannot address the needs you have identified in the sales conversation, enhance what you have said, or reassure that prospect you understand his requirements and problems.

**HELP HINT:** Following your sales letter, if you promised to telephone, reach for the diary and log it. You have left the door open, the prospect knows you will follow up, in fact, he will expect you to.

**HELP HINT:** If you use standard letters in your business, tear them up. They are no use to you at all as they do not target each prospect as an individual, but as a '*batch*'. People do not respond well to being pigeon-holed.

**HELP HINT**: The sales person who follows up, when he says he will, gets the business while the competitor down the road, doing the same job as you, may not.

It is possible that other people within the prospect company will see your correspondence and brochures, so your sales message infiltrates the organisation. It presents your image, and offers reasons why they should buy from you. Make sure it states the benefits of choosing you as supplier.

Some cold sellers prefer to send a letter first and follow up with a phone call. They are reassured that they are not going in completely cold, the ice will have been broken. But it won't be if the letter goes to the wrong person, sometimes the job title and the person responsible, are different. Much better to call first, get the right information from the telephonist, get through to the right person and sell. Put the phone down, and write a sales letter. Diary the follow up call.

You have spoken to the prospect and started a relationship so make the letter conversational, remembering people deal with people and your personality is important. You might risk some mild humour but you should retain a professional outlook on all dealings until you get to know the contact better.

**CAUTION**:    Never address a prospect by their Christian name until you know them. By opening, *'Dear Chris'* after just one phone call, you are being presumptive, not friendly.

Keep sentences and paragraphs short, restrict your points to one page and post it that evening. Use language the recipient can understand, you are not trying to impress him with words, but simple facts.

**CAUTION**:    Never use a word without knowing its meaning otherwise you might have tripped yourself up trying to be too clever.

It is not necessary to cram in every benefit or sales point, only those applicable to that client. You can deliver the others another time but for now, what he needs to know are sales points applicable to his need.

WHEN TO ENCLOSE A SALES LETTER?

Many clients ask if there is any need to enclose a letter when sending a mailshot. The answer is, always. It provides the opportunity to introduce the sales points of your product and although you will be talking to a general audience rather than a selected group, it is still an opportunity to highlight important points.

Mention brief details of any offer in the letter even though you might go into greater detail in a leaflet you could enclose. This makes sure the prospect sees the points even if they do not get as far as reading the leaflet in detail. The letter sets the scene and captures reader attention for the pack, providing it is not long and to the point.

## MARKETING METHOD NUMBER 8: COMMERCIAL PUBLICITY

*One of the 'advisors' mentioned in that chapter is the graphic design studio. It is surprising how many people have little idea what a graphic designer does or how to select and use one cost effectively.*

### HOW TO USE A GRAPHIC DESIGN STUDIO

There has been a revolution in the graphic design industry with the advent of desk top publishing (DTP) replacing the more traditional ways of typesetting by Linotype machine or lettraset on small jobs. The amount of work is much reduced and often clients do not understand the technicalities of design prices.

When selecting a studio, its representative should look businesslike. If they are too relaxed in their approach, they will concentrate their selling on how incredibly creative they are.

Creativity is something a design studio needs but **any** graphic designer can create a *'pretty picture'* as that is what they are trained to do. It is a different matter to apply **marketing** theory to the design requirement in order to produce your *'pretty picture',* but give the item the best chance of success by addressing the requirements of the marketplace.

A designer might create an innovative graphic with a stunning visual effect but if no one understands it, or what it means, the response rate may not be as high as if some measure of targeting goes into the design elements. The visual will capture attention but the sales message might be lost.

The way to compare studio costs is to ask for their DTP rate per hour, or if you wish, the studio rate per hour. This provides a comparison between contenders.

There are three categories of design firm. The first will need you to tell them exactly what you want, assuming you know. However when you do have an exact brief, they will come back with an exact translation.

The second category are those who listen to what you are telling them but what they produce has no relevance to the brief. The reason for this is that they put too much of their own creative thought into what you asked for. When you have given no instruction for this, it will waste considerable time in re-working visuals. The aim is the third category, a mixture of the *'translator'* and the *'creator'*, to follow your objectives without going over the creative top. You achieve this through thinking about your requirement, well before the first meeting. In practice, it is rare to find a client who has done so.

Some design studios don't ever have ideas of their own and expect to use yours. I call them *translators*. These studios are not good for progressing into your markets and you need to judge the value of this approach against your objectives.

To avoid these situations, you must make your requirements clear and it is advisable **always** to write a brief. The appendix has an example of a briefing format. This greatly assists the designer to produce visuals that are relevant and it helps you to understand what your requirements are. You cannot expect the designer to know anything about your product, company or market.

Your brief should cover the following headings giving as much information as you can:

•    *Item description, mailer, leaflet, brochure, advertisement etc.*

•    *Who will read it? (what type of company or person, what need do they have?)*

•    *What text will you use? (chapter headings to start with)*

•    *What visual images will you use? (photographs, cartoons or illustrations)*

•    *What are the sales points of the product? (You've got that list by now)*

•    *What supporting material can you supply? Do you have bromides of your logo to avoid them being regenerated, do you have competitors' examples to describe what you think will work, and what will not. Have you prepared a small visual of your own, however rough, to give them a start?* **See example in the appendix**.

**CAUTION**:    Get a firm quotation before you instruct the design studio to start. They sometimes work by preparing the quotation, then as alterations to the original specification are made, the invoice increases over the estimate. Insist from the outset that as the work progresses, anything not estimated before-hand or agreed in progress cannot be paid.

**CAUTION**:    Another area which can cause additional cost is *"author's corrections"*. You must remember that you are the author and if you change anything, the studio will take computer time to make your change. If you constantly change your mind during the work, costs will increase to a sizeable extent. This is another reason for deciding what you need at the outset and preparing a brief.

The difference between author's corrections and studio mistakes is a grey area and can lead to differences in your expectation of the final invoice. Sometimes, there can be good reasons for alterations from the original specification which can only be established as the work progresses.

- **IDEA**: List every single item where a change is made so as to be in a good position to discuss the final invoice. Agree with the studio where their mistakes have been made and where your change of mind has caused added cost. It is much easier to agree **as you go** rather than at the end when neither of you remember details clearly.

- **IDEA**: To avoid these difficulties, ask the studio to quote an all-inclusive price for the first job.

**CAUTION**: **Almost no one realises that settling the design studio's invoice does not mean you will subsequently own the copyrights of that item.** All copyrights are always owned by the originator. If you decide to change studios or have items prepared with a supplier other than the originator, make sure you have written confirmation of the transfer of copyrights to you before you do it. There is no defence to such an infringement.

Watch for items such as logos. It will take time and budget for a new studio to redraw them if you cannot supply a bromide. Always ensure you have lots of bromides of different sizes. If you are stuck, go back to some old artwork; you always have your letterhead which can be scanned.

- **IDEA**: Always ask for a bromide as a file copy of every project they produce. This serves as a record and visual reference to avoid work being done twice if you decide to change studios.

If a studio presents you with a colour laser visual, the item is stored as you see it on the hard disc of their computer. If this is the case and you need to make a few minor changes, that should not result in a big bill. The same is true when you have decided the final presentation and artwork needs to be produced. There is *almost* no such thing as artwork if all the initial work is done on computer and can be run out in reproduceable format such as bromide or film.

The page is generated or '*designed*' on the mac screen, the file saved to disk, the disk sent to the repro house who plan the film, scan in the pictures, drop them in place and then run out the final film. The printer makes plates from the film.

- **IDEA**: At the start of a project, make sure you have a complete understanding of the process and what the studio proposes to do for you. If you find a technicality you do not understand, ask if there are extra costs. The more you understand how they '*manufacture*' your requirement, the easier it is to control costs.

It is sensible to produce a rainbow or chromalin proof prior to printing, although it does create an additional cost. It is easy for small errors to creep in and for your own peace of mind, especially in a colour production, you should always check it before it goes to print. Laser printed copies often produce distorted colours.

The professional design studio can be an asset with the help and advice they provide. They should be able to apply marketing thought and creative promotional concepts and design at reasonable cost. They will have good communication with a client and being outside your industry, they should be innovative. Be sure to tell them what they need to know about your industry, so they can produce ideas suitable to your business. Show them competitor's examples.

They are not in your business, and so they will take an impartial view of your market. There are no politics or history; their ideas could increase market share, so develop a good rapport while you keep an eye on their costs. A friendly design studio is definitely an ally.

### THE CORPORATE IMAGE

*Your corporate image is the starting point for all publicity. How do you appear to the outside world? When did you last consider your image?*

It was Lady Thatcher who first brought the subject of '*design*' to the fore when trying to stimulate British business to sell overseas, and she was quite right to bring a measure of importance to how we look to the outside world.

Your letterhead makes the first impression on a prospect, new customer or supplier. Your corporate brochure should be sent with an accompanying letter. Your letterhead must be '*leading edge*' or your company, product or service will be perceived to be out dated.

Many MD's and owners were responsible for deciding on the company logo and layout which makes up the letterhead when the company started and naturally, they are proud of it. But if they are honest, can they claim that their letterheads portray a modern company, thrusting, vibrant and at the cutting edge? Probably not. How can they, if the design has not altered since the firm began?

It is hard to convince a chief executive who is emotionally attached to his ideas that the image the company portrays to the outside world is traditional, sometimes archaic, badly designed graphically, with poor colour combinations and retained for emotional reasons.

How many MD's know what is or is not a good image? How much PR could you get from a corporate update? It becomes a talking point and you can collect opinions. People think about your company again and what it stands for. Corporate image is the starting point in increasing awareness helping to win the customer's mind to think of you first.

A design studio should give you half a dozen ideas as finished colour visuals for under £500, less if you ask for '*scamps*'. Treat your image to an update. Recently, one client asked me if I had made a mistake in her estimate to redesign their corporate image. She had three quotes between £1000 - £14,000 and ours was £455 and included artwork. The studio charging £14,000 expected £5000 as a design fee. Whilst that is their skill, you can see how easy it is to be over charged.

- **IDEA**: Take a detached look at your letterhead from the customer's viewpoint. When was it last refreshed? Are there elements in it that were there when you started? Does it present the fashionable image for your market place?

In the section on tele-sales, I said that the first conversation should be followed up with a letter to confirm what was said, make sales points and establish what your next action will be. What happens if that essential follow up is presented on outdated letterhead? It will not instill confidence or say; *'You should use us as we are leaders in our field'.*

**HELP HINT**: Your modern corporate image should be everywhere - letterheads, compliment slips, business cards, the sides of vans, the front of the premises, the overalls and anywhere your company will be *'seen'.*

- **IDEA**: Start a design manual and set out the rules and guidelines for use, colour and positioning of your logo and company image. This might include your strapline or positioning statement as well. You should never allow these details to vary or be portrayed in a manner or place that could adversely affect your image.

**HELP HINT:** Always ensure all your publicity carries the corporate identity. This is absolutely critical in ensuring prospects and customers think of you before your competitor when they have a need. There is nothing worse than confusing your customers with 20 different images.

**THE VISUALS**

*Publicity starts with visuals.*

If you ask for *scamps*, the studio will return with rough sketches to talk around and this will save budget, although you do not get a *'finished'* representation of the item and you will need vision. If you request *visuals*, it should be a close representation of the final item.

This is a tricky time. At the first meeting, discuss a properly prepared brief, indicating if you require their creative input or a translation. The problem with some designers is, given a specific brief, they think they know better and return with ideas nowhere near what you wanted because they *"thought it looked better"*. This is their endless quest for a *"pretty picture"*, so you can see, it is vital to make absolutely clear what you want.

The key moment is when the visuals arrive. Whenever I present visuals, I always remind a client that their first impressions are extremely important. It is the only time you can be in complete sympathy with the people who will receive the finished publicity.

**HELP HINT**:   Make your decision at the first presentation, well before anyone else sees the visuals as that is the only time you will be able to experience an objective reaction, as your customer will. This is a clear case of first impressions counting.

Having seen all the options, you will doubtless show the designs to a number of people for their opinions: husbands or wives, suppliers, non-sales staff, in fact almost anyone who comes through the door. This can be damaging in the extreme as it colours your initial opinion.

At a recent presentation from eight very professional and *'finished'* examples, a clear favourite emerged and the client was very pleased.  I heard nothing for six months until a letter arrived saying that they could not agree on the right direction to follow out of the eight examples, and the exercise would have to be repeated. The outcome, a year after the presentation, was a plain coloured cover with the company name on the front, hardly a demonstration of leading edge technology to attract prospects in such a highly technical market place.

The client became totally confused and unable to make a rational decision from dozens of irrelevant opinions on what they **thought** he wanted - none of which were from customers, the recipients.  His sales team who desperately needed the item became more and more frustrated. Here was a clear case of letting other people's subjective opinions cloud the original requirements of the brief. Remember, your publicity has to make an impact at first sight and make the prospect react positively.

**HELP HINT**:   If there is a conflict on which text or design to choose or the correct way forward, the customer makes the decision. Answers to problems may be arrived at by asking, how can we best communicate the message to the customer and solicit the greatest reaction?

By all means listen to the opinions of others and hear what they say especially if they have more contact with customers than you do, but do not be swayed unless someone comes up with a valid objection that you had not thought of.  If there is any question, take the customer's point of view in making a judgement.

### WHAT IF THE IDEAS ARE "NO GOOD"?

In this context, it is important to decide what *'no good'* means. Does that mean you don't like the ideas?  While you and your staff should be comfortable in using the promotional item, your subjective opinion is less important than the opinion of a customer or prospect. Does it mean that it doesn't fulfill the brief?  Or more importantly, does it mean it won't work in the market place?

A competent design studio will look at your brief, discuss the finer points with you ensuring the full objectives are known and make absolutely sure what you mean.

When the visuals return, we have said your first impressions are critical. Argue for and against a design, not because you don't like green but because you are selling to a Far Eastern state where green might not go down well. It is common to listen to the Sales Director arguing with some passion for the blue design when the only criteria is, he likes blue.

**HELP HINT**:    Let the customer's likely opinion decide any issue that needs resolving as they are the ones that count in all matters promotional. This approach of taking the customer's viewpoint never fails in resolving any issue and it makes decisions much easier to reach as they are likely to be the right ones.

### VISUALS FOR NOTHING

*"Would it be better to ask 6 studios to prepare visuals for free so I can choose who I am going to use?"*

Do you get as good a job when you are not paying? Silly question isn't it? Take into account that a design studio has costs in preparing visuals. Many times, a prospect has asked me: *"You do a good job and if we like it, we'll pay you"*. If a studio accepts that challenge, in terms of quality of work, you will get exactly what you did not pay for.

***How many times this month have you agreed to give someone your product or service for free?***

The studio is in business to make a profit to survive, just like you and cannot count *'spec work'* as a major project *'in the bag'*. They will view your request as another prospective client wanting to see how good they are without paying attention to the skills demonstrated in their presentation portfolio.

The work will be fitted in around paying work and treated as second rate. The attitude will be *"Oh well, if we don't get it, there will be others"*. Requesting speculative visuals often means the client has gone to other studios all of them preparing visuals for free so the chances of landing the account becomes less.

A studio willing to undertake speculative work is sometimes one without work, which speaks for itself. Their creativity and ability to translate your brief into a successful promotional piece from which you can earn revenue should be their biggest asset. Giving it away without an agreed brief to work to speaks volumes about the overall ability of that studio.

Speculative work is counter productive to both parties indicating that the client has no idea what is needed and seeks to collect as many ideas as possible in the hope that something turns up and that it will work. The item selected from such an exercise will be the idea that appeals to the client rather than the market.

**HELP HINT**:   While you may think you are saving budget, you are not going to get the best ideas and much time will be wasted looking at everyone's speculative ideas, even the really bad ones. This makes reaching the right marketing decision even more difficult. The studio will be designing to please you rather than your customer which defeats the objective.

Where there is no brief, there can be no marketing input and what makes a promotional item *'good'* is if it *'works'*. If budgets are tight, ask for *'scamps'*. These are rough, unfinished sketches. Be prepared to pay something towards their preparation which can be negotiated. Invariably, designers will be willing to cover their costs without a huge profit if the studio schedule can cope with your work properly.

If you cannot assess their skills from past examples of their work, a trial job at a fixed cost is how you will get an idea of their capability. A couple of hundred pounds paid to three people will bring you a wealth of ideas and allow you to select the most suitable studio to work with. These may give you promotional ideas for future campaigns as well as the one you had in mind and thus, considerable extra sales.

## THE CORPORATE BROCHURE

Much depends on who you are and what your market place demands, but companies without an up-to-date corporate brochure, number in the minority. Members of your sales force or your sales representative will expect support material to be provided. After a meeting or presentation, something needs to be left behind with the prospect to continue the selling.

When prospecting a high level customer, at some stage of your presentation, they will expect you to produce your corporate *'glossy'*.

Research your prospects to find out what material they use to promote their own organisation before you make your presentation. What does their brochure look like? The more research you do in this area, the better prepared you will be, particularly if your publicity is not as good as theirs.

When presenting to a bigger company, it does not matter if your brochure is not as grand as theirs. Both sides know who has the greater budget. Following your sales presentation, internal discussions will continue with other colleagues who will need to be included in the selection process. Here, a well designed corporate brochure can be of great help in establishing who you are, what you do, how well you do it.

Later in the sales process, you may make a special proposal for that prospect, but initially, what do you have to impress them and encourage them to continue discussions? That is the main objective. So many brochures merely establish awareness of your existence and lose sight of the fact that they are sales documents designed to impress, establish reliability and success, continue the sales process, ending with a call to action.

**HELP HINT**: Your corporate brochure is a major sales document. Many smaller companies seek to compete using A5 or even DL size items. These smaller size items make good mailers but far from saving budget, these sizes are seen as coming from a small organisation and could lose you an opportunity. The perception of A4 size is far better and often masks your company size. Costs need not be prohibitive if you print a short run. Examine your sales presentation and use that as the basis for what you will say in your brochure.

Many clients I have worked with seem to have considerable difficulty in deciding the text for their corporate brochure. There are some general points you will want to make. More personal statements targeted to a particular prospect can be included in a covering letter or separate proposal document. If you are in doubt find a copywriter from Yellow Pages.

Your origins are not terribly interesting to a prospect although they do want to be reassured that you are reliable, solvent and not working out of the back of a rented garage. What you stand for today is what you are asking your prospect to buy. Put yourself in their position. What do you want them to know? What will win you their trust? What will convince them that you are of greater worth to them than the present supplier of that product or service? Where can you provide improvement to persuade them to change to your company?

Start with a description of the company followed by sales points for your products or services which apply to the needs of the market you have identified. The corporate brochure is a sales document, a selling tool, not an advertisement. It needs to attract, inform, impress. These are the ideas which the prospect needs to be reminded about when the sales person leaves, so make it a good basis for what you need to say.

- **IDEA**: Start by deciding chapter headings and add the points you wish to make in each section describing the various sales points. Only then, construct the whole text. Most people try to write the full text without a plan to work towards.

**CAUTION**: In deciding how to illustrate the text, you may consider cartooning which only works when it is done well and applies to a particular market or product. However, I usually advise against it as it can convey a flippant approach.

I have already mentioned that clipart is a give away for amateurism. Line drawn illustrations can be attractive and, after use in a brochure, could be framed and hung on the Chairman's wall as in one project I conducted, or used to welcome visitors in the prospect's reception area. But the usual choice is photographs, high quality from a library or from other sources, because they are relatively easy to obtain to fit the brief and are realistic.

My heart sinks when a client rushes to the filing cabinet to find the photographs he has taken. I have already said that none of us are experts in everything and most MD's are not professional photographers. Invariably, the quality of the exposure and the lack of experience in art direction is all too apparent. Sometimes, budget constraints mean they have to be used. Tact is required while the studio explains that it is very unfortunate but *"the photographs will not reproduce well in print"*.

**CAUTION**: Beware of the temptation to include a picture from a magazine or other published item. It is undoubtedly someone else's copyright. Every published picture is made up of dots. If you alter any aspect of that, particularly changing the size, you will affect the result. If you *'reorganise'* those dots in any way, perhaps by enlarging or reducing the size, you can get a ghosting effect known as a *'moire'* which ruins the picture with a damp looking haze.

The design of your brochure is important too, reflecting the way you do business. If your shop window to a prospect is old fashioned and not saying the right things, then it's definitely time to change it. A modern, smart and vibrant cover carrying few words, linking the design to your other promotional items, could be the key first steps towards winning a new account.

**HELP HINT:** Mention testimonial work where possible. A visual presentation, using a letter from a pleased customer describing good work you have done previously is a powerful way to sell your capability. It is realistic and allows the prospect to *'understand'* how you would approach his job.

Talk about the quality procedures you adopt to ensure that items delivered are correct. If you have unique selling points, explain them in detail. Often, a brochure text will major on what splendid service is *provided*, because no one can think of other areas in which they excel.

**CAUTION**: In situations like this, one hears the client saying, *"I want our logo and name on the front cover... probably doesn't need anything else?"* Even as a last resort, this is a lost opportunity. If you think back to advertising, why did I bother spending a chapter talking about the need for a good headline if it wasn't to capture attention and create a need?

If a prospect has not heard of you, your company name may not be enough to spark a need or capture attention.

Unless you are as well known as ICI, you are unlikely to gain much interest from your name. What will capture attention is what you do and how well you do it, not who you are. The use of your name alone on the front cover might suggest you have prepared it with *'you'* in mind rather than your customer.

Why are you preparing this promotional item, who is it for, who is it aimed at and how will it be used? Spare a thought for the prospects and customers who will be the recipients. Surely, they are entitled to a little more originality than a bare statement of your name and logo?

A demonstration of this comes from an unlikely source, a large metal recycling plant dependant upon engineering companies waste for its business. When this client decided to renew their corporate brochure, the front cover did not mention the company name. Instead, there was a splendid picture of a brand new BMW standing by a pile of engineering scrap with a large crane hanging above it.

The headline was *'Excellence in recycling.....'* which suggested their specialised line of business. It was a terrific photograph and the contrast of that gleaming new car against a pile of rust was dramatic. The brochure had an immediate impact and his customers were impressed as the photograph was much talked about for some time, going on to be used in advertising campaigns. This is an excellent way of capturing attention rather than by leading with a company name no one knows.

**HELP HINT**: If budgets are tight for preparation of a corporate piece, consider £1500 for 1000 copies in duo-tone, with pictures and text, A3 folded to A4 and printed on Conqueror high white laid board of 300 gsm thickness. That specification will make a perfectly good impression for a limited outlay.

Duo tone is a method of blending two colours, usually blue with black and using mono photographs to give a sort of *'blue sepia'* effect.

A designer is like an accountant. While using the service carries a cost, any advisor will produce a better result that you could have achieved on your own and save you costs as the project is executed. Use the advice you are given and listen carefully to what is said so that you can make proper judgements.

Like everything else in business, if time is at a premium, priority takes precedence and you must devote as much time as you can to understanding the various processes in producing this item so your judgement will be realistic.

## YOUR ANNUAL CATALOGUE

*Many businesses choose to publish a full catalogue of products either annually or bi annually and some industries design a completely new cover set for the catalogue, each time.*

Why are you spending considerable budget to have a new design on your catalogue covers every single year? Have you thought about it or do you change it annually because *"we've always done it like that"?*

There is only one reason to change covers and that is to show your customer a new look in the hope they will believe your products are new and to stimulate interest within your market.

You will need to change the message on the covers every three years or so to bring your catalogue up to the modern standards of design and colour and to take note of competitive activity. You may want to reposition the business and capture attention with a rethink inside and out, placing the products in a different order and using a new design inside as well.

But on an annual basis, a freshen up of your overall image is sufficient and can easily be achieved, keeping the basic image, refining the design and perhaps refreshing the colours. The budget saving will be considerable and that saving can then be allocated towards a totally new design in three years time.

Do you remember when Yellow Pages last changed their cover design? Quite apart from the cost of a new start, there is a significant disadvantage in changing every year. You may be jeopardising the recognition you have gained in the past year by a fundamental rethink.

Think of a shop window in your nearest High Street. The window itself does not change, the name of the shop is still at the top, the design is the same, the colours bordering the shop window are unaltered, it's recognisable. Now and then the shop display designers institute a different display theme, or change a few products to freshen things up and stimulate interest. The shop window itself doesn't change even though the features in the window may. My local John Lewis store has a big change of goods and colours on a monthly basis to create interest but the company name and colours never change.

> **Your customers will get used to the basic design.**
> **It is part of the conditioning process to win minds.**

Your catalogue is your shop window. What matters is that in customers minds, you are recognised by an established design. It is part of the thought process that wins the customers' mind. What is the point in starting all over again every year?

Another important point is that your whole range of publicity must look as if it has come from the same place. Many MD's do not recognise the need for the customer association that comes from a themed design across the range of all your publicity. If you are able to maintain the theme throughout, starting with the catalogue as the most prestigious item, then your customers will recognise you and associate your company with what you do.

- **IDEA**: Lay a sample of every piece of promotional literature you published last year on a table. Include everything, advertisements, leaflets, catalogues letterhead and see how different they are from each other. That is what your customers have received from you this year. How easy have you made it for those customers to appreciate that they all came from the same business?

- **IDEA**: Could your catalogue have some pages of local advertising stitched into the front and rear to provide an added service to those who read it and a small revenue to offset costs? If the advertisements are from non-competing businesses in the same market place, they will be produced for little cost if bromides or separations are supplied and whatever you will be able to charge for space will go towards the overall costs of production.

If you try this, start early so that you can work towards multiples of 4 x A4 sides and get a rate card drawn up to send to prospective advertisers to explain the idea, tell them the circulation, readership profile and indicate the benefits, the target market and how you will distribute the catalogue.

**CAUTION**: Your charge to the advertiser must include an allowance for the cost of producing the extra pages as well as a charge for the space on the page which you must cost out in multiples of four pages before arriving at your price per page rate. Remember too, there is a charge for binding the extra section, which could be printed by a different printer if it is cheaper for you, and then the printed sheets sent to the finisher who binds the catalogue.

## MARKETING METHOD NUMBER 9:     DISCOUNT BROCHURES.

*Terminology is important here. A "discount brochure" does not necessarily mean a brochure where product margins are slashed to pieces. Usually, it is a promotional piece which carries keen pricing, full of colour, movement and excitement to produce new buyers. Very much a prospecting tool, it has an application in most industries as it relies on low price perception in the mind of the customer.*

### *If your industry doesn't have one, this section in itself could make you money*

In some industries, monthly or quarterly discount brochures are published to sell product and create an upward curve on the sales graph. Their major function is to quote good value offers, in order to open new accounts.

Sometimes, they are used to '*sell up*' and introduce a wider range of products to present customers, but trading an upward sales move for reduced margins is not exactly the right idea when the real objective is to open new doors. To capture new accounts, you need very keen pricing. When the door is open, it is a common tactic to increase your margins and extend your range.

Getting those new accounts with a high value, low price-perceived discount brochure or short order catalogue is the best way to cover a large number of prospects in the hope of establishing them as regular, new customers.

The most widely known of these is the stationery brochure sent out by Viking office products of America. Since they arrived in the UK, they are reputed to have taken some £250m away from our commercial stationery suppliers by appealing to a sector of the market ignored by much of the UK stationery industry - the growing, emerging and recently established businesses which comprise some 94.6% of the total UK commercial population.

The company launched by utilising a new marketing technique I call '***mailswamp***'. Far from getting one brochure a month, Viking sent five or six in the hope they were passed round your office and given to business colleagues.

They targeted every small business in Britain, which our commercial stationers would never see as a cost-effective market. They bought every known mailing list and applied an amazing budget. The product quality was good, the prices were reasonable and the items arrived the next day. No argument at all if you were not satisfied, back it went for a full refund or replacement.

Irwin Helford, US Chairman of Viking, the one on the front cover who then called himself the more British "*Ian*", admits at speaking engagements in the UK that he sells on price perception. If people *think* the price is low, they buy.

In fact, the price is very low in your first copy of his brochure but they soon rise, so much so that he is reputed to make at least 40% GP across the board which on £250m, even after the cost of mail swamping is a healthy return. Increased prices are not exactly a reward for becoming a good customer and most Viking customers probably do not realise the prices change and just carry on ordering.

Supporting my point about changing catalogue covers, Viking's brochure hasn't changed since inception because it does not need to when the objective has always been to establish it as leader in that market place and when *mailswamp* is used as the method of distribution. Products look good but the text is very wordy and sometimes, the prices are hard to work out.

Viking has captured the minds of many buyers who think they're the cheapest and no longer bother to check to see if they are. Viking makes the purchasing process very easy and the easier you make it for your customer to buy from you, the less the customer thinks about changing supplier.

To a marketing man, it was fascinating to see the entire industry seized with panic. Every discount brochure in the stationery trade changed design by varying degrees, adopting features from Viking's design, employing tinted boxes for product backgrounds. This was despite the fact that the success was not coming from the design, but the method they used; precise targeting of an unserved market using perceived value, *'swamping'* and providing the small business with an extremely good service not generally available to that market segment.

What is interesting is why commercial stationers or buying groups in the UK, having lost so much revenue, have chosen not to mimic Viking's market-swamping approach on a local basis in their own area. How easy to do the same, mailing discount brochures to small businesses, offering the same range of products, immediate delivery if the order is big enough, which in a local area, could be done with little difficulty.

Another sales advantage when competing with Viking might be that you are British. Viking is not, and it has been proved that as a nation, we are quite willing to support our own manufacturers. Those old enough will remember the *'Buy British'* campaign which worked well for a long time until cheaper foreign imports arrived *'en mass'* and British goods gained a reputation for poor quality in comparison. Whilst one can only admire Viking's achievements in the UK, and now France and Germany as well, it could be that the issue of nationality is their competitive Achilles heel.

It is a fact of life in a small business that to establish a discount catalogue in an industry unused to this form of marketing will take a large budget. Yet there is no need to devote millions as in Viking's case. There would be a number of industries able to increase sales by preparing their own version of a discount catalogue.

The shelving or racking industry is another example of an industry where discount catalogues are commonplace, with three major suppliers each of whom employ different types of catalogue with varying degrees of success.

If you are trying to convince people that your business offers good value when comparing quality against price, then prices do have to be good. Working on the theory of *"pile 'em high, sell 'em cheap"*, you are trying to sell more product at a reduced margin, so reduce your margin or buy better. Can manufacturers help you with special prices while you try this new way to increase sales levels?

The designs within the brochure, as well as the covers have to be very clear and look as if they are changing with each issue, even though the products inside are substantially the same. Discounts as high as **50%** or **60%** off recommended retail price should feature frequently and use **70%** off, or above, for the front cover. It is not much of an incentive to talk about saving -5% or -10% unless you are talking in retail terms.

- **IDEA**: Could you set up a small localised *'Viking-type'* mailing operation in your area? It is a simple process with the aid of Kelly's directory to create a list of small firms and mail them on a frequent basis. Do not fall into the trap of sending a catalogue which is a reference book not designed to sell products off the page.

Make the design colourful, exciting, full of information as well as containing *'offers'*. Offers do not necessarily mean low margin products, but well-designed pages selling hard, featuring the benefits of each product, how they fulfill a need, allowing the customer to perceive good value. Always offer a gift on the front cover for orders over say, a £50 level for instance, to increase or establish a high order value. You will find people make up their orders to gain the benefit. Be sure to include an order form and put the size-of-order-incentive clearly on the order form.

Discount brochures are a successful form of marketing. Are they used in your industry? Could your's be the first?

## MARKETING METHOD NUMBER 10:       FLYERS

*Otherwise known as leaflets, flyers can have a dramatic effect in producing an upward turn in sales enquiries, depending upon their use.*

If you use them as inserts in magazines, it is claimed you can expect a 2% increase on advertisement response levels as more are '*noticed*'. Using colour leaflets, A4 printed one side can be powerful.

Used as mailers, a flyer can often produce a sale at a time of year when sales are slow.

### SEVEN DAY MADNESS

One client always had a poor August and a hopeless December. I invented a flyer called '*7 Day Madness*' with a cartoon of a crazed individual, hair on end, and shouting about four products which were at lunatic prices for the next seven days only. It went out with an order form.

Not only did sales of those four products reach all time records but including the other items sold by tele-sales staff, the first August was a record month that year. Obviously, it was not a good plan to do it again in September as it would lose '*bite*' but each December and August, the 7 day madness leaflet featured as a regular part of the marketing plan.

The policy of using four products was forcefully argued against by one MD I worked for. *"Given a blank back, why can't I use it and why can't we feature six or eight products on the front cover?"*

The answer is, you can, and testing will tell whether it is a good idea. By featuring a low number, you draw interest to those few products and provoke a fast reaction as customers stock up. We did try five more on the back and an order form and it was more productive. Obviously, the origination and print cost was higher using two sides.

It is not always advisable to fill up every last centimetre of white space on a flyer. Often, much more impact can be gained from using the white space to allow the message to stand out. Using white space gives a production a smarter appearance as well.

By restricting the number of products featured, you '*stock up*' customers using those products that otherwise might be sold to customers by competitors. I call this process **"*stacking out*"**. The success of this marketing route depends on the pricing, promotion and advertising which is decided by planning and testing.

I have enough copier paper in my building to last for at least eight months thanks to a local flyer promotion that offered two for the price of one, the old retail technique of *"buy one, get one free"*. They held on to the second load until I needed it, overcoming the storage problem and the whole order worked out to a very respectable price per ream.

In the normal way, I would never have contemplated buying so much. A splendid piece of marketing and one that could work well for you. Obviously, with such a large stock now, I would not contemplate ordering from a competitor for a long time. If their systems of checking customer satisfaction levels and retaining customer loyalty are efficient, I might never change supplier.

- **IDEA**: Can you think of two or three products that you could feature at great value prices to '*stack out*' against a competitor? Your buying terms should be better if you order a greater quantity and with only three products, you may secure help with your promotion from a manufacturer to make it even more profitable.

Royal Mail has recently begun a new service of leaflet distribution door to door, that takes away much of the wastage since the days when young lads were employed to do the job.

The Royal Mail certifies delivery numbers and costs at present are quite reasonable at £40 per thousand. This service cannot be split between commercial '*drops*' and residential, the only selection criteria being by postcode. If you know the post code of an industrial estate or your town centre, you can be fairly sure your flyers will reach businesses. Tell Royal Mail which postcodes you want and they will tell you how many flyers they will need. A leaflet ideally with a letter and a reply mechanism or a coupon is the best way to break into a new account.

- **IDEA**: Call your local Royal Mail sorting office and ask for the telephone number of the Royal Mail business centre who will be able to give you the details of all services designed to help businesses together with costs and arrangements. Try distributing 1000 pieces to local businesses and test the reaction.

- **IDEA**: When your goods are delivered, they go directly to the person who uses them, not the buyer or specifier. Delivery is a unique time to talk directly to your end user. So put one or more advertising leaflets into each delivery. A leaflet containing different offers reaches the consumer in a delivery box, an excellent time to sell more.

- **IDEA**: Use a loyalty scheme to encourage customers to come back to you. You may feature a slow moving range to clear it or a very profitable range. It is a good time to prepare a small card which carries your logo, telephone number and positioning statement just to say "THANK YOU". Now there's a novel idea.

*When did you last thank a customer for trading with you?*

- **IDEA**: **GET PAID FASTER**.....Why not institute a system to ensure that every time you receive a cheque from a customer, you send a compliment slip saying, *"Your cheque arrived safely today; thank you for trading with us. We will be in contact with you shortly."*

Add the names of members of your staff who transacted the order, particularly a sales person in day-to-day contact with that customer. How's that for service, courtesy and being different from the competition?

There are very good reasons to consider this idea. Fostering goodwill is an important one, but so is showing your buyer how long it takes for you to be paid and this can be a good opportunity for you to improve your cashflow.

It is not usual to invoice until completion. Given a sixty day, average credit period, that means your '*thank you*' note could reach your contact some ten weeks after the work was complete. Often, this is a surprise for the buyer to realise how long after completion payment arrives, and on the next negotiation, you could suggest he asks the accounts department to bring your payment forward which might help your cashflow. You may gain status as a favoured supplier to be paid preferentially. You are more likely to achieve a good result this way than if you asked his accounts department directly.

Some businesses continue to send leaflets with Statements which go into the accounts department rather than the buyer's office. Invoices, on the other hand may or may not go directly to the buyer for approval prior to payment.

While it is likely that anything the buyer receives which is for accounts eventually gets to accounts, it seems rather unlikely that sales material would get back to the buyer. As a small business myself, I open all the mail and I have to confess to disposing of leaflets which arrive with invoices or statements as I am more interested in the figures than sales messages.

## MARKETING METHOD NUMBER 11:        NEWSLETTERS

*How many times have you received a newsletter and wondered if this method would help your business? Newsletters are one of the simplest and most beneficial ways to publicise your company and stay in touch with your customers. Yet few businesses seem to issue them, possibly due to worries of lack of material.*

As usual, in a business context, this is not rational thought. It goes without saying we are all busy, but if newsletters are an item which can work for you, then preparation becomes a priority and other work should be held up while the newsletter is prepared. There are not many forms of promotion or advertising where you can act as an editor and say exactly what you wish to a captured audience.

Commercially, newsletters are a valuable opportunity to remind customers and prospects of your activities, informing them of developments in your industry or your company and providing a means of increasing communication to strengthen relationships. It also serves to sell products from advertisements you might include as a space filler.

A newsletter should never need to be withdrawn for lack of content. How many people work in your firm? How many staff, suppliers or advisers do you have? All these people can be asked to contribute a small item every month, quite apart from what **you** can say.

The material must be relevant rather than explaining which washing powder Betty in accounts favours or the score at the darts match last night. A newsletter provides an opportunity to re-state sales points and provide testimonials or case studies which sell for you as well. For general interest, workers can talk about their jobs. Some personal items do *'lighten'* the read but that should not dominate content, nor should competitions and games although these items can add interest.

For most people, asking for a contribution will not be onerous; it should involve all levels of staff, working as a team. It will bring a diversity of interest to the paper and ensure that you never miss a quarter for want of material. Snippets can be adapted to suit your business from other Newsletters, and course notes, items of a general nature may come from friends and colleagues in other industries, although you must be cautious of copyright issues. As a last resort, a trained PR professional can be called in to finish a floundering issue.

Managers at branch offices of national companies could use information from other locations. The fact that an article was published in the Leeds branch newsletter does not limit use anywhere else in the UK. Branch offices have no excuse for running out of material which can be *'traded'* with colleagues.

- **IDEA**: Here is another example of networking with other businesses. How many companies are there in your immediate area with whom you could exchange newsletter articles, thereby adding interest and helping each other?

It is best to begin with quarterly issues, until the amount of material supply is assessed. Start collecting material well before the first issue. The size of typed text invariably takes more space than the final edition.

Using as little as 10 point is perfectly readable in a newsletter and anything left over can go into the next issue. Even 9 point, as in this sentence, is acceptable especially when the text is in a column.

If you can afford full colour and A3 size, (twice your letterhead paper), it will add to the professional appearance of your company.

- **IDEA**: If news is scarce this month, consider adding advertisements for your products to fill the space. Make the offers individual to that issue and not available elsewhere. That way, you have a measure of their effectiveness.

- **IDEA**: Get one of your manufacturers to *'do a piece'* on his process. Every manufacturer will appreciate the added exposure for his products and may even be willing to sponsor that page or pay for the insertion. They might offer you a special promotion or better buying terms on the product featured.

- **IDEA**: Write down all the things you could tell your customers about your business, the products, staff, delivery methods, the process or recent large orders you have fulfilled successfully. Write some articles, don't worry about the English, there are plenty of people to help you with that. Can you think of interesting things about your industry that your consumers may not be aware of? It doesn't matter how long or short the articles are. Put it together, cut and paste onto an A3 size sheet and fold it in half. Think of a name and you have your first issue, have it printed and get it into circulation.

One client publishes his monthly newsletter to customers, not to disseminate *'news'* about his company, although it does that on the front and back covers, but to make sales from the editorial and products featured. He puts in formal adverts when they run out of editorial material. It has opportunities for prospecting too and the beauty of a newsletter is that you can write what you like.

Newsletters have many uses. Our local pub has a *'regular'* with some time on his hands who writes a one sided sheet called *'The Whistler'* that appears in a special holder on the bar each Friday. It contains local gossip, stories related by people in the Pub and interesting snippets about the landlord and clientele. It is surprising how early the bar fills on Fridays with people calling in to see if they are featured in the columns that week.

- **IDEA**: Competitions add sparkle. Publish a photograph of a member of management at the age of 6 and ask customers to guess who it is for a bottle of Champagne. Publicise the winner in the next issue. It adds interest.

- **IDEA**: Create a crossword from features of your product or service. For an anniversary edition, one client drew up a structure chart showing the dates of service of each person and asked one question, *"What is common about our people"*. The service of each member of the department added up to the length of time the company had been established which could be worked out from the structure chart.

- **IDEA**: Send a memo to each member of staff, supplier and manufacturer you deal with, explaining that you are considering publishing a newsletter and could they supply some copy. Ask for sponsorship at the same time.

- **IDEA**: In a commercial business, a newsletter is a splendid way to keep in touch with customers, feature prestige jobs you have completed, and carry testimonials from clients you have 'interviewed'.

- **IDEA**: Your newsletter can carry features on members of your staff and what they do, who they are, what their interests are.

- **IDEA**: A newsletter is a good way to undertake a survey and publish the results.

## SUMMARY

- Choose products to promote in the newsletter and make some special offers.

- If you start a newsletter, in the second edition enclose a questionnaire to see what your customers think of it.

- Pick out some key prospects and write a letter asking if they would like to be placed on your mailing list to receive your newsletters on a regular basis.

- Plan a response chart to record the product sales that come directly from the newsletter.

## MARKETING METHOD NUMBER 12:        FAXSHOTS

*Personally, I could never recommend using this marketing method to promote as there is a widespread loathing at receiving them, but many businesses are presumably using faxshots to good effect.*

More traditional ways of promotion do not carry the stigma of the faxshot, which uses a customer's paper and equipment to deliver your unsolicited sales message. This adverse reputation seems to be much greater than when I was developing the telex medium for advertising purposes.  Then, there were a few complaints at first, and telex numbers were instantly erased.  Now, the reaction is more intense and modern automatic technology frequently delivers a number of copies of the same thing.

However, like everything else in marketing faxshots do have a use.  They are cheap to despatch overnight in large quantities and many companies provide a commercial service broadcasting faxes for small sums.

I would never risk upsetting a potential customer unless testing had proved beyond doubt they were in a tiny minority and the system does produce positive results. But I would be cautious.

Where faxshots fall down is that the ***personal*** aspect is lost.  As with all mailing theory, if you can appeal to individuals on a personal level, you will gain more attention by better targeting, and so it is with faxing.

•        **IDEA**: A far better way to conduct a faxshot programme is to use it during the daytime to highly targeted individuals as a matter of business, making it look '*normal*' rather than a distribution to 1000 others at the same time.

•        **IDEA**:  Always show full reply addresses, telephone and fax numbers so if someone wants to complain, they can.  Establish a procedure to handle complaints and if you have purchased a list of numbers, make sure the originator is informed of anyone not wishing to receive broadcast faxes.  That way you can demonstrate a caring service and retain your reputation.

Any company that does not publish telephone and fax numbers or does not respond to faxed requests asking for fax numbers to be deleted, are guilty of an uncaring attitude towards prospects.

- **<u>IDEA</u>**: With larger companies allocating fax numbers dedicated to particular departments and sections, there is now a way for your daytime communication to reach a prospect in a large company. In the past, the telephone or a letter have been the only way and both have barriers. Faxes are delivered and read so do not abuse the facility by a blatant advertisement.

- **<u>IDEA</u>**: When you are asked to *'send us the details'* at the end of a tele-sales conversation faxing them can be very effective as they will reach the contact quickly who maybe elusive to other sales approaches by mail or telephone.

If you are an incensed recipient of an overnight un-requested broadcast fax, under the Data Protection Act you can ask for information held about you on the sender's computer to be given to you. This is an irritant and as an alternative the sender may be more willing to have your number eliminated.

Companies who use faxshots may not realise their action could alienate consumers and this is not something I would encourage my clients to risk. Some company buyers prepare *'blacklists'* of companies using faxing to sell, the method is **that** unpopular.

Researching the method for this book, I received a letter to confirm the removal of my number but what a waste of a sales opportunity. Not one person I complained to ever telephoned personally to apologise or try to overcome the objection and sell me their goods. Certainly I would have taken the call had I been telephoned and tele-sales people will tell you that reaching the correct contact is the hardest part of their job.

- **<u>IDEA</u>**: My solicitor recently pointed out that it is a legal requirement, not widely known, that any business communication must carry the company registration number of that business. It is good advice to anyone using the method, to include it.

Using the untargeted *'shotgun'* approach which could alienate consumers is not a method I feel comfortable with recommending, but if you do not have my reservations, conduct your programme professionally, and be aware of the fact that there may be many prospects who hold my view.

## MARKETING METHOD NUMBER 13:                    PUBLIC RELATIONS

*An important part of the marketing mix is keeping maximum customer awareness. The more you tell, the more you sell and it is worth taking time to consider this section.*

PR is a function which has responsibility within the business for all dealings with the outside world, how the company is represented, what should be said to the Press, anywhere the company comes into contact with the public, their customers or suppliers. In large organisations, the PR dept will vet everything, brochure text, end of year results, newsletters, anything which might be said by the company, about the company.  They are total protectors of the *'spoken image'*. Some people even extend that to checking replies to letters of complaint.

In the PR department of one large client, the first two hours is spent making cuttings from all the newspapers of that day, read previously by members of the department on the train coming into work. These cuttings are compiled and on Director's desks by 9.00 am and report anything *'said'* about the group or their competitors in that day's papers such is the importance placed on what is said about the company by others.

Traditionally, in commercial organisations of small or medium size, PR has been seen as a means for a company to gain awareness as Press Releases are sent out and followed up and relationships with editors fostered. Where there is no formal PR department, the function is left to a busy manager with other priorities.

Keeping customers and prospects informed of *'what's happening'*, new product launches, new markets opened up or even a very big, or technical job completed successfully for a big name customer can get you exposure.  Good *'raw news'* works much better than the myth of expensive lunches for editors.

Press Releases to trade magazines often result in sales enquiries. They may be few, but will be of **very high quality indeed** far exceeding that of response from advertising.  You are better placed than anyone to form a close working relationship with your trade magazine editorial team who have the power to help you in spreading the word about your business.  It is possible to create a good relationship where they can trust you to supply newsworthy items.

**HELP HINT:**   Regular releases take thought.  Every trade magazine prepares a list of features they intend to publish in the future and this means you can tailor your release to fit the feature. The features list changes from time to time so you need to keep in touch with the editorial team and adjust your schedule accordingly.

Certain features may offer good advertising possibilities too, and remember, the editor works a long way ahead so if you do have an appropriate press release, send it in early, marked for that edition, and check that it is received.

Always work ahead of time when preparing Press Releases. Every time you issue one, you should have the next one prepared and two or three ideas to follow up with. That way, you feed through a continuous stream of newsworthy items, create opportunities to talk with the media, strengthen relationships and improve your overall exposure.

The way you present a news release is important. Press releases should be short and to the point, with a photograph included and always followed up by telephone to ensure receipt. Enquire as to whether more information or explanation is needed.

**HELP HINT**:  If you send a photograph, try to be sure there are people in it. So often, the imposing new front entrance shows no people. People add interest and give readers something that they can identify with.

**HELP HINT**:  Make sure photographs are clearly captioned, not with a ball point pen but with plain paper and Pritt stick. You cannot publish a photograph that has a heavy line embossed from the reverse.

Ideally press releases should have their own headed paper with the words "**News Release**" in large letters on the top. The 'story' should be written in double line spacing allowing for editor's comments to his production team and at the bottom, a name and telephone number for more information.

When submitting Press Releases, remember the difference between advertising and editorial. In an advertisement where you pay for the space, you can say what you like as long as it is *legal, honest, decent and truthful.* Editorial though, has to be interesting, objective, impartial, and a news item or feature piece carries the editor's endorsement. They do not need you to '*write*' the article but they do need you to tell them all about it, so present them with the facts.

Read your trade press. Get to know what sort of stories are given prominence and how they are written. As with all promotion, write the story from the reader's point of view, not yours. Always get a second opinion on the worth of your story - is it really newsworthy? Ask a journalist on your trade magazine as they are the best judges.

When news is slow, editors might be interested in items on promotional or charity events, staff stories and achievements, sponsorships, staff promotions or retirements, long service awards, community service items, anniversaries, new or refurbished premises or facilities. These subjects, however, are peripheral to the main purpose of the publication, even though they may be the most important thing to happen in your business.

Find out when the deadline is so you know the time factor involved in reaching a particular issue. Whenever possible, give advance notice of a forthcoming event as a story arriving out of the blue on deadline day will not endear you to the editor and reduces the chances of the piece being used.

Don't assume everything you send will be used as it is the editor's choice, not yours. If it fails, carry on with the programme, revamp it to make it more newsworthy and bring it back later, re-written of course. If you do get a call to phone back, DO IT, and at the agreed time. One failure on your part shows unreliability against other news-providing sources.

**HELP HINT**:   Always follow up every release with a phone call. *"Did you get it, is there anything I can explain, do you need to know more about any part of it, do you think you can use it?"* The more you build the relationship, the more they will come to know you are genuine and not a time-waster.

Good press relations are self-generating. The more you keep in touch with your trade press the more they will rely on, and use you, which means your business will be featured regularly and lead you towards the goal of becoming a local industry institution.

Invite a member of the Press to visit you, take photographs and write an article about your business, your process or your product. Are you having a business function which the Press could attend? Your local radio station may well be interested in looking at what you do and this will reach business people as well as regular listeners.

It is worth checking all the business media available in your trading area. Local exposure can be an excellent motivator for your staff.

The relevant issue of BRAD, mentioned in the advertising section of this book, is available from your local library and features business publications circulating in your area that you may not know about.

**HELP HINT**:   Any publication will send you a media pack on request which will include samples of the magazine and data on reader profile, circulation, features and so on.

Your main target is the trade press titles which appeal to your industry but you may gain exposure in other media. It is worth contacting the business section of your local paper, not necessarily published each week, monthly regional interest magazines and other county business magazines. Chambers of Commerce often have publications which circulate among the business community.

While they represent less reader coverage to potential customers, these magazines are often stuck for general interest material and will sometimes respond to an interesting release, especially if your business is '*local*'. You must decide the worth of talking to them as regularly as to your trade press, but it costs very little to keep them on the PR mailing list. Every published story that appears increases awareness of your products and your company.

- **<u>IDEA</u>**: List all the facts that might make a newsworthy story in your trade magazine. Think of personal aspects about the business, product reviews, anything a manufacturer has done with one of your products that you can highlight. EC directives needing explanation to your public and customer stories about the large, technical or difficult orders you have fulfilled, can provide material.

PR is a versatile, cost effective means of communication, providing sales leads of good quality if not quantity. It provides you with the means to reach a wide audience. It can enhance the reputation of your business, build on that reputation and hopefully, bring you more customers. It should be part of the overall marketing mix in any business, and if you cannot cope with such a sustained programme in-house, a PR professional will always talk to you, tailoring their charges to your firm's budget.

## MARKETING METHOD NUMBER 14:        EXHIBITIONS

*For small companies, exhibitions can be one of the most expensive items in the marketing plan because you have to cover the cost of the stand space **and** the display material. When you add the costs of stand staff and their hotel expenses, the decision to attend becomes very important. It is critical to get the maximum sales out of the show which is difficult if you do not have the time to prepare properly.*

### WHY ATTEND?

One reason given for attending a show is, '*we always go there*' and amazingly, exhibition stand space is often the first thing written into a marketing plan. However, the reasons **why** a company attends may not be given annual consideration.

Many companies exhibit because if they are not there, everyone will think they are in trouble. I cannot count the number of times I have heard that statement. Yet in isolation, it is the least important reason to commit such a large amount of budget.

Invariably it is the competition, rather than the potential customer who will believe you are in trouble. If you decide not to attend and this possible reaction concerns you, mounting promotions around the time of the show can help to demonstrate you are still active. An ordinary promotional mailing to all customers and prospects is one strategy. Rational explanation to anyone who asks gives the opportunity to explain that costs are rising and some things are just not worthwhile. A customer will understand that from his own experience, and any conversation with a prospect or a customer is another opportunity to sell. However, you should promote to sell more, not appease the opinion of the competition.

> ### As a small or medium sized company, assess the likely outcome
> ### rather than the tradition.

The decision to exhibit or not needs careful thought on each occasion and the decision should be based on likely results. First, look at the measure of response and conversion to sales you have enjoyed year on year. Do you make sales at the show? If you do not, and if no sales or very few come from show contacts, then a return visit really does need a closer look. Could the budget be allocated in a better way? Have you had more success in a different area, for example tele-sales, or mailings? Would it be better to allocate the show budget to what is already working and producing?

If you can justify the cost, exhibitions are a unique opportunity to meet prospects face-to-face, to sell and to take orders. Once again, I have had clients who do not see it that way. Presumably they think that attendance is a total PR exercise and an opportunity to tell as many people as possible what they are about. While that's true, it should also be a way to make a sale.

Recently I went to assess the stand of one of my clients which had become unproductive against the cost. The stand staff were talking to a few people occasionally. After looking at and adjusting the layout, I asked, *"How many orders have you taken?"* *"None"* was the answer. *"Why not?"* I asked. *"Well we are only here to meet people,"* came the reply.

I put a clip board in the MD's hand with a standard order form on it and gave my opinion. By the end of the show, they had four signed orders and 20 future appointments, one from a multi-national they had been trying to break into for months. They had simply forgotten that they attend shows to make sales rather than just collect sales enquiries for afterwards and increase awareness.

- **IDEA**: Does your company regularly attend a show? When it is discussed at the next meeting, shock everyone by asking why you go? If it is to sell goods or services, how well did you do last time? What sort of increase do you expect on that figure in % terms? How are you going to achieve it and what resources do you need on the stand to make the new target?

As with most marketing, you have to look carefully at which exhibitions present the best potential for you. For seven years, ours was the only design studio to attend the Direct Marketing Fair, and we obtained all our prospect business for the year, with no other promotion needed. Perhaps that was lucky, but the Exhibition Bulletin lists every single exhibition taking place in the UK and Europe. Select one to suit you.

Having decided to attend, the budget question looms again when ordering space and deciding the position of the stand. It is imperative to see a return in results from that allocation.

### DESIGNING THE STAND.

Free standing space, the big stands on plinths, are usually occupied by the large players in the industry who really are there *'to be seen'* and can allocate the requisite budgets. One stand I planned and mounted for Courtaulds, attracted attention when a helicopter was flown into the NEC and wheeled onto the stand. This captured more visitors than ever before. The helicopter came free in exchange for allowing a name board of the aviation supplier and a sales person to be present just in case. It was a good example of business networking. There were over 400 enquiries for Courtauld's products and three enquiries for helicopters!

Small and medium sized companies will be jockeying for the shell scheme areas around the hall. Once again, in planning how much space to take, decide the objective, the target market you want to try to attract and *then* the available space. A very common error is to book the space first and then decide what you will do with it .

The haste in booking may be due to the pressure of the exhibition organisers pushing to sell all the space in the fastest possible time to capture the income and maximise their bank interest before they have to make payments. You are the customer so be aware that when the organisers call, their objective is to allocate all the space as fast as possible and your planning decisions must be made promptly.

Shell scheme space needs careful thought both in the planning and the siting. You may not think so judging by some you will see. Usually it is better to be close to a tea and coffee area than to an entrance. In the main, most visitors do walk around the whole exhibition anyway, the only place they tend to linger is around the refreshment or bar areas.

**HELP HINT:**    Having chosen the site, decide which way the main pedestrian flow is moving and put your primary graphic display facing that direction.

- **IDEA**:   Stand layout is critical to achieving your objective. If you are at a show for three or four days, try a new layout each day. Have you ever seen anyone do that? It is a splendid time for **testing** and apart from a little thought and some planning, *there is no cost* attached to this idea.

Staff do need to sit down from time to time, however, the stand is not a resting place but one where business is transacted. Make the stand unthreatening and uncluttered with tables and chairs. Staff can always go to a coffee stand or bar with a good prospect and sit down there or even somewhere previously reconnoitered outside the exhibition hall. That can save budget as then, there is no need to provide other than basic, on-stand catering, if at all.

Do you want to restrict the amount of literature disseminated or is the objective to get your details in front of as many people as possible? Answering that question decides how materials will be distributed around the stand and the best place to position stand fixtures.

- **IDEA**:   Remember to ask the organiser if they supply the visitor list **after** the show to put onto a follow-up, mailing database? If not, how will you arrange to collect names and addresses from people who come to the exhibition?

- **IDEA**:   The collection of names and addresses of visitors is paramount to post-show follow up so you must collect them. Why not mount a business card draw for champagne or a special competition prize by business card.

- **IDEA**:   Most people forget that last year's visitor list might still be available. You could send an invitation to every one who attended last year and hopefully produce an increased number of visitors to your stand this year. Offer them a special gift to be collected from your stand and do not offer the gift in any other promotion, while the show is on.

144

Obviously, the more people you can talk to, qualify, sell to and sign up, the more cost-effective your exhibition becomes.

Will you clad the shell scheme with graphic panels? It is an expensive outlay at first but if it is a worthwhile annual event, will amortize over subsequent years and the effect looks professional. With subtle changes, three years is a reasonable life. You do not need to change your corporate brochure or catalogue cover each year to maximise your image in the customer's mind, so why bother with an annual re-design of the exhibition stand?

Cladding the upper half of each wall with graphics is quite reasonable in terms of cost and effect. Although not as professional looking as a full cladding of the walls, your designer will still have a large area to use for a graphic to attract passers by. Beware of items not the width of the panel wall, stuck on at infrequent intervals with velcro showing lots of blue stand material bordering the graphics. It looks very *'home made'* and not the image one should portray.

Some changes of colour, with new panels for new products or other significant services, is all that is needed. Cladding the walls using 5mm foamex, heat sealed and fixed with velcro will last 3 years, or longer if handled very carefully, especially if the corners are protected. Liberal bubble wrapping will keep them clean and hopefully, undamaged.

**HELP HINT**:   Never go to an exhibition without a box of supplies including male and female velcro, scissors, sticky tape, plasters, aspirins, a black marker pen and a felt tip pen. It is amazing the things one is asked for by fellow exhibitors and there may be many minor changes you might want to make to your stand once you see it assembled.

STAND ETIQUETTE.

Exhibiting can be the most wearing, boring job in the world and staff need frequent breaks and something to do that doesn't look unprofessional when the delegates are in their seminars. I well remember learning the Morse code one year without any idea when I might need it.

Will your stand have chairs? If the answer is yes, will the staff sit on them more than the prospects? Chairs on a stand are an invitation to bad form. Are you there for a fireside chat or to do some serious business? If staff need to sit down, they should go off the stand to another location. They should do so if they need to eat or drink. There is nothing worse than an interested prospect, waiting to ask some questions but not wishing to upset the staff break. Staff on stands often look and act as if the stand area is part of their own home, a restricted area that they would prefer no one else invade.

Sometimes, personal belongings within the stand area such as briefcases are enough to reflect a less than professional image - can't they be hidden? Raucous laughter, in-house huddles, guarded conversations, all seek to exclude the prospect who might have come a long way to see your company and will feel intimidated.

People who walk the halls find it difficult to break into a pre-existing group. But they may have big budgets and you don't know who they are, what they need or how much they are prepared to allocate to your company until you have asked them. So treat everyone in a friendly, fellow-professional, welcoming, helpful and efficient manner.

**HELP HINT:** It is quite common for students to tour shows collecting brochures. While these may be read, they will never be used for their prime purpose of selling. A useful tip is to ask anyone enquiring for a brochure to let you have their business card. More names and addresses are collected and this excludes students who never have one. Growing businesses have to think of the expense of brochures so leave it to the big boys to look after the students as they can afford to.

• **IDEA:** If there are few visitors around at certain times, face half of the staff on the stand inward and half outward so, it appears one section is talking to the other. You'll be surprised how people suddenly become interested in your stand when they think others are.

**SELLING FROM THE STAND.**

A walk down Petticoat Lane in London on a Sunday morning will teach you the rudiments of crowd gathering and selling to a large number of people. It is creating this crowd which is the secret of successful exhibitions and the more people on your stand, the more people will come on to your stand.

What is your objective in being there? Do you expect to sell, collect names and addresses and distribute literature? If so, you need people on your stand. How can you draw a crowd? One company at the Direct Marketing Fair each year used a roulette table with free chips on presentation of your business card. If you go to the Travel Trade Show, you will see fire eaters, jugglers, magicians and a number of scantily clad young ladies distributing leaflets and gifts in the aisles. These strategies are affected by budget, aesthetics and by how you wish your company to be represented.

It could be argued that the roulette table is just a bit of fun. It might be frowned upon by some. Only you can gauge how your prospect public will think of you and whether there is any risk to your image.

- **IDEA**: Take a look in the Exhibition Bulletin and select a show similar to the one you usually attend. By similar, I mean a business-to-business selling show rather than a consumer one. Look around the hall, carefully noting what people are doing, what they are attracted to, which stands are doing best, what they look like, how the graphics are used.

*There is absolutely nothing wrong with attending a show to get some ideas.*

- **IDEA**: At the end of the day, you need people to sell to and if they won't come to you, go out into the aisle area and get them. Direct approaches are always the best, depending upon how it is done. If you just thrust a leaflet at someone and ask; *"Would you like one?"* they may take it to get rid of you but it is hardly selling. Involve people in a conversation. Open up with a question. *"How many pressure boilers does your company use?"* or *"Do you need a plastic bag to carry that lot? - have one of ours?"* There are lots of ways and that is what sales people are good at.

- **IDEA**: If you are depending on the show to distribute your leaflets or brochures, place the literature rack at the end of one of your walls with the length parallel to the back wall, **not** up against a side wall. That way, it masks off a third of the space where the staff can stand and this arrangement offers a prospect an unthreatening open area, where they will not be pounced on, and which is *'safe'* to enter. Of course, as soon as someone moves forward to take a leaflet, one of your staff should run out from behind saying; *"Have you got the correct one for your needs?"* and then on to what their needs are and into the sales patter.

*Do the preparation again, even if you have been a dozen times*
*before and measure results against costs.*

### FOLLOW UP.

- Preparation includes how you will cope with the *'whole'* response when you return to the office, not just the hot leads. Over time, you could probably **double the business** from your exhibition by handling it better upon your return.

- During the exhibition, call into the organiser's office to see if you can order the visitor list when the show is over.

## MARKETING METHOD NUMBER 15:        BREAKFAST SEMINARS

*More companies are considering the use of breakfast seminars to sell to specialist or larger buyers. This is another relatively new way to market your company with greater impact for a small outlay.*

In the section on Exhibitions, I discussed the ways you could organise your stand to create a situation in which it is comfortable for your prospective customers to talk, face to face, the very best way for selling.

Most business people do not mind getting up early to attend a presentation and breakfast at a central hotel where parking is not a problem. Often, this is preferable to a lunch where costly, dead travelling time is greater and one is not likely to be back in the office before 3.00 pm. With getting to and from a business lunch taken into account, half the day is gone.

The format for a breakfast meeting starts with coffee and a personal welcome at 8.00 am by one of the host staff, a presentation in a formal situation starting at 8.30 am, using overhead projectors or video, a question session, an information pack and then on to breakfast at around 9.30 am.

During the meal, the selling is done seated at circular tables with two host staff allocated to each. Breakfast needs to be of good quality with options for vegetarians and those who prefer low fat diets. No one thinks of low fat food and it is vital for individual needs to be catered for in confidence, so that all guests feel comfortable.

Unless they have a *real* problem, guests do not expect alcohol which is a definite cost and sales reason to choose breakfast rather than lunch. It is quite amazing how intimate such an event can become with prospects listening to each other's questions and subtle selling taking place.

Equally important is the opportunity to follow up with a, *"Did you enjoy it?"* and *"Will you find it useful?"* follow up call.

*   **IDEA**: Does this have an application in your company? Highly targetable, it could be a much better way than your traditional *'road show'* format? With the number of EC directives flooding out of Brussels, there should be no problem with subject matter.

Breakfast seminars are ideal for new product launches, new systems, and new factories or products, as well as breaking into much larger customers as supplier. I know of one organisation that mounted a breakfast seminar for all the potential high spending accounts in that area and were unashamed at quoting the reason for the gathering - *'to win big new business'*. This was achieved.

Breakfast Seminars can pose a problem for competitors who might like to do the same but won't want to be seen to be copying.

If your company needs larger customers to help it to grow, invite a chosen number of contacts to your premises. If those are not suitable, a local Hotel, or a room at your local Chamber of Commerce building to try this very simple form of marketing will impress prospects and put them at ease.

Be sure to have the requisite amount of promotional material available for each delegate to take away with them as well as carefully following each one up, preferably by one of the sales people they met on the day.

## MARKETING METHOD NUMBER 16:     EDUCATION SEMINARS

*Depending upon the length of time you have been trading, you may have a wealth of knowledge within your business. Telling people what you know can be a very successful marketing method.*

If you have the subject matter to be interesting and informative, this method could represent an excellent sales opportunity.

When this book was first written, I was a member of a networking organisation, The Business Network, which held lunches all over the UK where business people came together to do business with each other at monthly lunches.

The system was excellent, very professional against competitors and I managed to 'befriend' a number of the *'hosts'* requesting 20 minutes to make a presentation on marketing and at the end, to mention my book. I sold 163 copies that way from the first 15 lunches and ended up covering most of the UK very successfully.

As a result of these events, I was asked to return to run a two hour workshop. At another lunch, a delegate offered to put the book on the Internet for a small commission and at yet another, a local paper agreed to run a reader offer using the book. These initiatives were very successful.

In your business, there may be technical matters, EC directives, even general information which could be of use to prospective customers. Running workshops or seminars captures your audience for that period of time, impresses them with the depth of your knowledge and offers the opportunity to present your company as a prime mover in your industry.

Speaking engagements are becoming more popular with the advent of business breakfast clubs and networking and I have listened to some inspiring speakers on all sorts of topics. Once you have perfected your rendition, see how many people will allow you to present it. The Chamber of Commerce is a good start as they are often involved with various business functions which need speakers.

One organisation holds regular seminars lasting three hours and include a number of excellent informative sections even though the MD is the first to admit it is done to sell his company. He now charges over £50 to attend because at lower levels, people did not see the worth and stayed away. Is this an idea for your company? Your local Hotel will be pleased to quote for a room, regardless of the size of audience.

**MARKETING METHOD NUMBER 17:**      **COMMERCIAL POINT OF SALE**

*Selling business to business, point of sale is vital. Invariably, it is the point where the person who uses your services has the first contact with your business, as opposed to the person who specifies or buys them. What opportunity might this present?*

In a retail sense, point of sale is very important in presenting a potential customer with a suggestion to buy through a sale sign, a price discount sign, a product benefit notice and so on.

But, it is so easy to forget that the object of point of sale material is to *'sell at the point of sale'* and there is an application in commercial terms here too. Fortnum and Mason send out all their goods in boxes sealed with printed, sticky tape which carries their name.

When your goods are delivered to the customer, are they in a custom pack, or an old cardboard box? Do they have tape round the package with your logo and show your positioning statement and telephone number? Do you put leaflets into the package providing the customer with other opportunities to buy goods from you at a special discount? Do you ever say thank you to a customer or user for buying from you? Do you ever ask that your company be specified next time?

The important point is that delivery may be the only time you are able to reach the end user, the consumer of your product with whom you might never communicate, if your usual contact is the buyer.

In large commercial organisations, the purchasing is done by the buying department responsible for achieving the best continuing value for their company. It could help you to initiate a favourable conversation between the buyer and the end user in the hope that your products will be specified next time there is a need. The publicity you enclose with that delivery becomes critical to that process and this is a way to sell which is not open to competition. Make sure that you ask for your goods to be specified, as your call to action.

The point of sale is often the point when a commercial customer sees the goods he or she ordered, for the first time. Might you be missing opportunities?

## MARKETING METHOD NUMBER 18: TESTIMONIAL PROMOTING

*This is an under-utilised marketing method which involves ways of getting your present customers to tell your prospect customers how brilliant you are. It is a definite and serious method of growing your business if you concentrate on the "bigger" end of your market, the prospects with big budgets.*

If you ask, many customers are happy to provide you with a letter saying how well you did. Testimonial letters rarely come unsolicited but if you have done a good job for someone, it pays to ask them to drop you a line, and say so.

These letters seek to persuade prospects, using live situations, that your company has done well. They can be used in newsletters or mailers as long as your customer does not mind and it is most important to ask him first.

- **IDEA**: On a regular basis do you ask for testimonials from customers who are pleased with you? They will be flattered to be asked.

Brochures carry the logo of clients or customers who use your service and visually, these can be very powerful indeed in persuading others to allow you the chance to serve them. Once again, you need written permission otherwise, you will infringe a copyright.

The wall of my meeting room is covered with forty testimonial letters collected over the last 20 years, from happy clients reflecting continuing good service. I let them '*sell*' for me by allowing a prospect to spend a couple of minutes exposed to them while attending to the coffee. When I rejoin the client, they are studiously reading them one by one. The same is true when interviewing new suppliers.

### A PROSPEROUS DAY OUT.

The big, corporate sector is particularly difficult to break into. It is hard to dislodge competitors hungry for large slabs of business and willing to cut prices to the bone. Another good example of testimonial promotion is illustrated by a company already serving some large customers, but with the capacity to serve more. The main stay of their message was the excellence of the attention they pay to customer service and they have made a science of it.

The company decided to try a form of testimonial promoting, an innovative method where you use one customer to attract another and their tactic was a specially prepared golf day. To begin with, the course was the best, Wentworth. Teams of four were made up of one customer, two prospects and a salesman, teeing off for a good days' golf. Can you imagine what four people will talk about during eighteen holes? Well, that was what the salesman was there for, of course.

Following the round of golf came a sumptuous lunch, not a normal business lunch but a £50 per head meal. Again, plans had been made carefully with the seating order following the pattern of one customer, one salesman, one prospect. In the evening, during dinner, there was an award ceremony for the highest team score.

Not unnaturally, there are no publicised results from such a gathering but as an important example of planning and execution, could they have done anything other than very well indeed? In fact they must have, as the event takes place four times a year.

This story has relevance to a smaller business. You may not be able to afford the budget to emulate their activity but on the other hand, it could be that this method has appeal and you might decide to sink half the annual budget on a similar event, perhaps on a smaller scale.

There is nothing wrong with that, but it is absolutely critical that the approach works. That means unplanned promoting is strictly out. Consult colleagues about the idea and get views from outside, small business people who might help with contacts or hints.

One way to guard against a total failure is to follow up; *"Good morning George, I hope you got home safely. Did you enjoy yesterday?"* That should be one of fifty calls you make the next day, followed by fifty the day after and so on, not forgetting that the object is to take your sales process forward one more level, not only to chat with George about the day but moving him on to the possibility of new business.

## MARKETING METHOD NUMBER 19:    PRODUCT CARDS

*You must have seen little packs of postcard-size product cards in your pile of mail? Some clients swear by them as a reliable source of sales leads and there is no doubt that given adequate research into who receives them, they may well provide you with a highly targeted medium.*

Their strength is in the speed in which a recipient can assess your message and the fact that while your advertisement appears on the front, a reply address appears on the back. By filling in the form and dropping it in the post tray, responding is made very easy. As with any form of advertising and promotion, the faster and easier you make it for respondents to get back to you, the better.

It is not widely realised that the cards are produced by trade magazine publishers and as such, can be duplicates of advertising placed in magazines although there are some produced by special publishers not affiliated to magazines.

The cards provide another way for readers to be presented with your sales message and given that they are an immediate response vehicle, they could prove productive.

As a reinforcement of your message, they have a use. However, unless your budget can stand advertising exposure by both magazine page and the product card, try testing each method in turn to see which works best. Three months in the magazine followed by three months on the cards seems quite sensible or if budget allows, both together. Product cards are usually published quarterly.

There are independent publishers of product cards who research lists of recipients and in this case, targeting is far better and much more likely to prove useful in providing your business with a new advertising medium.

- **IDEA**:   Talk to other advertisers who appear in the product card pack you are thinking of entering. Give them a call to see how it works for them. Is the publisher a magazine or an independent? Both can be good but the independent list may be stronger, if the respondents have asked to be sent cards, rather than the magazine using its circulation list.

**HELP HINT**:   If you are selling direct to a particular industry, call the trade magazines and see if they publish product cards. Look in BRAD, *British Rates and Data* where product card distributors can be found under your industry.

## MARKETING METHOD NUMBER 20:     SPONSORSHIP

*The Nationwide Building Society recently announced an agreement to sponsor what we all know now as 'the Endesleigh league' for a reputed £5 million. An investment of such a huge sum can only be made because the company expects to get the investment back, and more. Why else would they spend that much money? What relevance has this for your small business at a local level?*

The exposure to be gained by Nationwide nationally over the next 3 years is colossal, as their name will appear on television wherever the league is featured. Clearly they must see the expense as retrievable.

There are two real advantages to taking a local interest.

1.       Visibility amongst your prospects.  If you sent a mailer to a good prospect and on Saturday, he goes to watch the local lad's football team sponsored by your company, he will identify with you, and repetition sells.

### People buy from people.

2.       The reputation your company will enjoy.  People will know of you and want to work for you.  If quality staff are easier to find because they know you and what a good firm you are, then costs in finding them are reduced. Most businesses are only as good as their staff and *staff* in this context are best drawn from the local area.

Although it is difficult to measure, local sponsorship can be an effective way of keeping your name prominent.  Sponsorship takes many forms from paying for the horticultural tent at the village fete in return for some free advertising, to sponsoring the kit of the local basketball team or under 15's football.

Rather than just a name on the programme, print a voucher that people have to post back to you to receive a gift.  Once again, that provides a direct measure of response.

The object of sponsorship is gaining maximum exposure for your company, product name, strapline, even telephone number, to the exclusion of your competitors.  It is a far better investment than that offered by a trade magazine asking for £50 in order to appear in a Christmas crossword competition they are running.

In assessing the value of continuing sponsorship next year, measure the results against cost in terms of keeping you in the public eye and the '*worth*' that provides in raising awareness.

## MARKETING METHOD NUMBER 21:     ELECTRONIC CATALOGUES

*Technology is moving towards an electronic purchasing age where everyone browses, selects and pays on line. The first tentative step on the road towards full EDI (electronic data interchange) or full on line trading is converting your brochure or catalogue to an electronic catalogue.*

To this end, many companies have developed electronic catalogues of varying quality where part of a catalogue can be scanned and pricing details added. The whole item is then put on disk or a CD for use on a client's own computer. In this way, even if you and your customer are not fully integrated on-line, at least an order can be printed and faxed, sometimes directly from the PC. All such orders will comprise standard layouts that you can understand and use quickly.

Electronic trading is a very important advance which seems to have been greatly overlooked, mainly because businesses do not realise the immense benefit of *'locking'* a customer into a supplier who provides this advantage.

The first stage, the electronic catalogue provides the customer with a fast modern way to select products, produce an order and send it to you quickly for rapid despatch of your goods. To the supplier, your customer is *'captured'* and the medium is excellent for selling.

The orders you receive in this way will be in the format you need for full efficiency and can claim priority. A group I work for uses this approach and has now developed their Windows version and locked in customers all over the country, providing PC support and upgrades to maintain interest. In addition, those customers enjoy a special *'efficiency discount'* not available to anyone else which creates the aura of a built-in loyalty scheme.

- **IDEA**: If you read an advertisement in your trade press or anywhere which offers a demonstration disc of an electronic catalogue, send for it and look over it carefully as it could have an application in your business.

It is not a complicated matter to develop an electronic catalogue. Many computer consultants listed in Yellow Pages have the necessary experience and can quote for the development work based on using a database programme like dBASE or Foxpro. If you cannot find a suitable supplier, call the helpline number which can be found at the back of this book.

## MARKETING METHOD NUMBER 22:  ALTERNATIVE BRANDING

*A marketing tactic for selling more of the same product is alternative branding which often takes the form of 'second branding' or developing your 'own brand products'.*

### SECOND BRANDING

Many growing companies may not have considered how easy it is to develop a second brand. If you manufacture the goods or services you sell, second branding means putting a new package around the same or a very similar product, calling it something different, repricing and selling it into the same market.

Given the ability to package as you wish, another option is to sell along side yourself. In other words, you compete with yourself, in the same market, with almost the same product, but sold in a different, unassociated pack.

Consumers develop a brand awareness and affinity based on advertising and use. In such cases, you may well see a buyer maintain a strong purchasing preference for one brand against another when in fact, both come from the same source. You could find yourself in a market served by four products where two are yours, with a subsequent increase in profit.

-  **IDEA**: Look at your range of products and see if it is possible to arrange to supply a second brand to sell alongside your present brand. The second brand may be '*an economy version*' of the same item or a product you choose to sell at a lower price. Equally, a more expensive brand which carries extra value for the customer can create more profit in selling almost the same product at a higher price, as this has the effect of protecting the brand you now stock.

### OWN BRANDING

*Own branding is similar in concept, the difference being that the second brand openly carries your identity. Own branded product which can be sold at a premium price now accounts for 36% of all products sold in the UK.*

You may know that many large supermarket chains sell cornflakes in their own packs which sometimes look a great deal like that of the independent brand leader. Kellogs highly value their quality and go to great pains to point out that they do not make cornflakes for anyone else.

In this way, supermarkets offer their *own brand* cornflakes at a discounted price with goods of a lesser quality. Their overall market share is greater and their margins are the same since they appeal to upper and lower end consumer demand.

- **IDEA**: Are you in a market that could stand another brand? Do you manufacture, import or sell anything you could conceivably put into a new pack? Would you be better with your *own brand* or competing directly with your present product?

Obviously, this is a complex subject and involves major decisions but it offers an excellent opportunity to extend your profits. By raising or lowering the product quality to satisfy a second consumer need, you may reach new customers not previously available.

## REPOSITIONING

*It is possible to increase sales and profits with the same product or service but by creating a different appeal.*

Repositioning is common and many companies look at traditional markets to decide whether a *'shift of emphasis'* might increase sales and profits. Sales may be markedly higher by using research results to relaunch, with newly designed packaging targeting a different category of customer.

A local Church held a *'Carols evening'* for a number of years which included a dinner and entertainment. Numbers gradually dwindled and discussion led to a change of venue, a new title, *'A Christmas Candlelight dinner'*, and a higher price. The food and entertainment was the same and the new event was over subscribed. People's perception of the event altered to make it more appealing to those who knew it as well as attracting a wider customer base.

I was asked by a client to advise on increasing the sales of their magazines. Little research had been conducted but various promotions had been mounted with poor results. Examining the target market, I found that more people bought the magazine directly than purchased from bookshops. The client agreed to a large investment in a survey from the present readership, to reorganise the design and layout and adopt a radical new cover. The promotional budget was reallocated towards direct sales. New subscriptions were taken out, more customers were attracted by the redesigned contents and higher sales were achieved.

It is true that a product reposition can be costly and unless based on research, there is a risk. However, in a traditional market where sales are flat or declining, take time to think of ways to spark a greater interest from present customers and the attraction of new customers, which may create a sales increase.

## SUMMARY

- Research the market to see what consumers want and then see if you can fulfill the need in a different way with alternative branding. If you find demand, talk to manufacturers about developing your own packaging.

## MARKETING METHOD NUMBER 23:        THE CORPORATE VIDEO

*Research in the UK regarding the effectiveness of video over the printed word showed that 82% of the sample found it easier to comprehend.*

### WHY A VIDEO?

For a small or medium sized business, whether providing a product or service, this form of communication is a worthwhile contender for some of the promotional budget.  Admittedly a video is a big expense with costs of approximately £1200-£1500 per broadcast minute, depending upon how much location work is required against using a recording studio or your premises.

It is easy to spend that amount in one year on advertising and the chapter on that subject will show how there are ways to waste that budget if promotional activity is squandered or badly executed.

Video costs can be kept down and one client I advised made a good saving on average production costs when I suggested choosing location shots close to home and preparing the script to avoid lengthy and costly post-production editing work.  The cost for twelve minutes was only £8000.

Remember **people will watch it**.  Your message will reach the target, and used wisely, there is no doubt that a well produced corporate video can be of assistance in spreading your message. It will impress prospective customers who have the ability to place bigger orders than you may be accustomed to, especially in a new business pitch where the competition may not use video.

This makes a video an important marketing resource, if you are seeking to grow by expanding your average order size. A small company grows by sustaining product quality, giving consistently good service and with sufficient financial reserve to be able to transact more business from larger customers. Given that you prepare a corporate video, sales presentations to larger prospects suddenly become possible. A video comprises good material suitable for a breakfast seminar presentation to a number of '*larger*' prospects.

But how do you secure the attention of that prospect with bigger purchasing power who is difficult to impress, especially if your company is '*small*' in comparison?  The key point is, it is watched.  Even though a prospect knows it is going to contain elements that '*sell to him*', he will still watch it, probably at home in a relaxed atmosphere, without interruption.

## VIDEO - THE CONTENT.

Unlike the corporate glossy, the reason for considering a video in the first place is not just to be seen to impress. Video should convey action and movement in presenting your company. The classic van shots coming out of your factory or warehouse implying orders flowing out to customers are more dramatic if the vehicles are moving. They are less impressive static.

If your manufacturing process is intricate or you have just equipped a new despatch area with live racking, showing the baskets travelling two miles collecting various parts of the order, ending up with quality control is *interesting* while at the same time, *selling*. It is the element of movement which creates the interest.

Video allows you to let a '*presenter*' do your talking for you, a professional approach which will convey your message. The presenter leads the viewer through the process to the conclusion which is always the same - we want your business. It can be dramatically effective, and interviews with you and other key people along the way can make sales points in the strongest possible manner while still being subtle. Video lends itself to the most powerful form of testimonial promotion.

If it is planned carefully, various items such as new product introductions, enlarged or improved facilities can be '*stripped in*' later in an editing suite, at any time after the original was shot. But things change, and sometimes, because of the location of the original shoot, a whole sequence needs replanning and reshooting.

## THE ENDING - CLOSING THE SALE

A factor consistently overlooked in a corporate video is the ending. Some come to a close with a musical fanfare, the presenter almost shouting about the company and summarising what has been said. To my mind, that is not the best way to end, although a summary can be helpful.

The conclusion should be your reason for producing the video in the first place. Some sales people are not good at asking for the order and sometimes forget. You cannot end by saying bluntly; "*Now you have seen what we can do, you really should call us*", although that **is** what you wish to convey. Thus the final section needs careful thought.

In all selling situations, your success rate will improve if you have targeted closely and planned how to counter objections, deciding what your strategic approach will be. So it is with the end sequence of your video. Will your audience allow you to ask for an order at this stage or must that be done face-to-face rather than on film?

You must clearly demonstrate the commitment of all the staff to service providing '*service*' is your principle, and is articulated throughout the company.

For example, if the video is to be used at live presentations, you might end with;

> *"We hope we have convinced you of our capability and we want to do business with you. We want to continue discussions and our staff are on hand now to answer your questions. Thank you for the time you have taken to learn more about XYZ. We look forward to doing business with you."*
> (Ends)

When the lights go on, someone springs up and says again, thank you for watching, do you have any questions? In other words, the presentation continues where the film leaves off and the process is planned to lead to asking for their order.

A video can lead on to wherever you wish, which a corporate brochure can not. Obviously, the video must be adaptable for watching in home situations as well as in a presentation. Some companies make two or three endings for use in different selling situations.

<u>CHAPTER 4</u>
<u>MARKETING FACTORS FOR CONSIDERATION</u>

*These items are not planning 'fundamentals' but areas that every business needs to look at carefully when planning and undertaking promotions. This chapter could provide the fastest way to increase your net profit.*

## LAPSED CUSTOMERS

*Lapsed customers can often be your fastest source of instant profit. They have dealt with you before, they appreciate your ethos and standards of service but for a variety of reasons, they have not bought from you recently. Do you know who they are? How can you find out? What might be the extent of your loss if you take no action?*

The trouble with customers who '*lapse*' is that they decide to buy elsewhere or worse, they do not tell you why they stopped buying from you. It is easy to be so busy that you do not notice you are about to lose their business. How long do you give it before coming to the conclusion they are '*lost*'?

There you are, serving them and without warning, they receive a better offer from a competitor. Before you know it, they are gone. The operative phrase here is '*before you know it*' because unless you have already recognised this problem and instituted a system to catch those potential lost sales, you will lose their business. Precious budget has then to be devoted towards trying to win them back.

We are talking of previously regular, satisfied customers who have not purchased from you recently. Lapsed customers are easily identified from computer reports or record cards, even manually from sales ledger sheets and they can be a good source of quick, extra sales and profits.

My car was serviced by the same garage for three years when I became irritated with the proprietor who would call me exactly thirty-one days after rendering his invoice, complaining that his terms were strictly thirty days. I was not avoiding him, just busy. Another garage had been mailing me, it was less expensive and I decided to try them. Ten thousand miles later, the first chap called me to ask if I had missed a service and by that time, I had become a firm customer elsewhere. Had he known of my anticipated defection sooner, or checked my satisfaction level, he may have been able to talk me round or make me an offer to retain my business.

Your computer report that identifies this sector should be run every month with programmes constructed to retrieve the suspected lapsed accounts well before they are '*lost*' rather than '*lapsed*'. You have to decide the period between sales that you will classify as the '*lapsed period*', it may be three months, it might be longer.

That way, you can take steps to retain the vast majority of business you have. You can catch anyone who may move away from your products by taking immediate action to identify who they are and act to keep or retrieve the account.

### CAN YOU CATCH LAPSED CUSTOMERS BEFORE THEY BECOME LOST?

It is worth repeating a recent example from my client casebook used in a previous chapter in case it was missed, showing the sort of problem that may be encountered and to the surprise of this MD, the extent of his potential loss, and yours if you are not careful.

The client had all his customers and prospects on a computer database. I suggested that a search should be undertaken to find out how many customers had not made a purchase during the last three months and what they had actually purchased in the same three months last year to assess the extent of the possible lost sales.

It transpired that out of 2200 customers on the database, 600 had not made a recent purchase. During the same period last year, those 600 customers accounted for turnover worth £90,000. If that client did not contact each of those customers, probably with some form of offer to attract them back then £90k was the potential, overall loss to that business. With this startling fact brought to light it would have been simple to construct a mailing programme with tele-sales back-up and target to recover half the potential loss at least. The Boss said they were too busy. This is a genuine example.

- **IDEA**: Run a computer report, as the client in the example did, to discover how much your business might lose this month. This idea alone had the potential to make the client in the example £90,000's worth of **EXTRA** turnover.

### SUMMARY

- Remember lapsed customers, one of the fastest sources of new profits. Call and say; *"We haven't done business with you recently, is there a problem or have we let you down in any way?"* Remind them of your continuing good service. The chances are high they had forgotten you and you will take an order. WITHOUT THAT CALL, YOU MAY HAVE LOST AN ORDER.

- If the idea makes sense when applied to your business, could you run a system to produce a report every month as a check?

- If you do not operate with computerised accounts, look through the sales ledger and isolate those customers who have not been invoiced during the last three months. It will be time-consuming but given that information, you can see what you might have lost.

- Set up a programme to attack these accounts quickly. Will you use tele-sales, mailings or another method to bring customers back before the competitors lock them in?

## NETWORKING

*A recent business development has been the emergence of what are called, "networks". These revolve around lunches or other gatherings where local business people meet to present their businesses in the hope of making useful contacts. Everyone knows why everyone else is there so the pressure is off.*

Apart from gaining more customers, these gatherings can be useful in developing relations with local businesses that might assist yours by way of joint marketing, shared databases and mailings, or even use of your showroom for a business activity. You never know what relationship might result and as a recent idea, networks are a superb way to establish and maintain business relationships, promoting helpful contacts as well as increasing sales.

Co-operation with a car dealer who wants to display one of his cars on your premises, reciprocated by taking a space in his showroom for your products, could bring profitable new business for both and increased interest for customers not expecting to see another firm's product range. Daewoo cars, the dealer-less, direct car sales manufacturer are hungry for sites from which to sell their cars.

Some Chambers of Commerce are mounting successful gatherings of small businesses wishing to trade together. Some run the functions at cost which makes the idea of networking very cost effective but business clubs that stage good speakers sometimes do not have the emphasis on doing business. Sometimes, even non-Chamber members are welcome.

The major private network nationally, which is highly recommended in forming these relationships, is called '*The Business Network*'. This organisation is eight years old, has 10,000 members worldwide and they have created local networking areas around the UK centered on major towns. Their method of working is professional, up-front and well planned; a relaxing, free drink for those who want it before lunch, exchange of business cards, a three minute presentation from table members and various interludes to create selling situations. Each month, you sit with a different group, the lunch is of a high standard and ends promptly at 2.00 pm. The tables have no more than eight people, all of whom are MD's or decision makers, all there intent on trading together.

These lunches take place each month in a comfortable hotel or other well chosen venue and that allows for discussion after the lunch for anyone wishing to develop a relationship further. Your more forward thinking competitors are probably already there.

- **IDEA**: Check with your local Chamber of Commerce to see if they stage network lunches. The Business Network can be reached through 01992 500 530. It could be the best thing you ever did in promoting your business to others in a similar situation to you.

## DIRECT

*Commercial companies who send out promotional literature need to be mindful of the power of one word in the mind of any consumer. The word is 'DIRECT'. What does that immediately mean to you? No middle man = might well be cheaper?*

In retailing, this idea from the US is gaining interest with those retailers who constantly need to attract consumers looking for bargains - and these days, who isn't? Once again, there is a message for businesses selling to other businesses here too.

The *direct factory outlet* for instance has totally transformed the well known Galleria Shopping Centre in Hatfield, just North of London. Built for £145 million, ten years ago as South Hertfordshire's West End, the local council tried to protect the town centre by restricting all the usual high street retailers who would traditionally be invited to open new stores in a development designed to sell to well-to-do North Londoners. In short, other retailers were not forthcoming in the required numbers and The Galleria went bust. It was sold to an American consortium for £12 million who proceeded to establish *direct* factory outlets in the vacant space and have been eminently successful selling seconds, discounted lines and previous sale items, *"direct"*. The Centre is now invariably packed with people at weekends looking for bargains, when before, it was empty.

The commercial lesson here, is in attracting new customers apparently with incredible deals that give the impression they are going to continue for ever, and that savings come from the apparent absence of the middle man.

Already mentioned in this context is the very successful Viking office products company who send you two or three discount brochures with incredible prices, and as soon as you buy from them, these prices disappear and everything goes up. Commercial companies selling to other commercial companies need to emulate this marketing idea where possible.

By instituting a level of publicity at the *'factory outlet level'*, I will call it the *'DIRECT'* level, prospective customers may be persuaded to give you a try. The *Direct* item, which is purely for opening new doors, carries a small range of products. Assuming your business supplies everyday products to industry, a small number such as fifty, depending upon your range, might be very heavily discounted. As soon as they buy, a new customer goes onto the higher level discount brochure which nets you say, 40% GP and offers a greater range of goods, probably 200 - 300, all fully guaranteed and delivered next day where possible.

Look at this marketing method which gains new customers by instituting low price/high-benefit publicity to attract new customers. Then, when they buy, transfer them to another brochure with higher prices but which also provides greater perceived value while it increases your margins.

This was the strategy I proposed to one of my clients who's sales people had mistakenly distributed their discount brochure to present customers as well as new prospects. The brochure prices were low to attract new customers and this reduced margins. Gradually, prices crept up and so the brochure became much less successful in opening doors and a new prospecting vehicle was needed.

The dilemma was, with customers used to the item and buying from it, it could hardly be cancelled so I suggested a sheet we called XYZ Direct, where XYZ was the client's name. It was smaller than the brochure, an A2 sheet folded to A4 carrying just fifty prime, everyday products, heavily discounted. This corrected the situation and produced a far happier sales force with something to go out and sell with.

When promoting with more than one set of prices, it is critical to ensure that anything with lower margins does not reach an established customer. Given a sensible attitude and full understanding of the objectives, lower prices mean more doors will open - the object of the exercise.

## TIME MANAGEMENT

Bill Gates, Chairman of Microsoft, said on Radio 4 recently:

*"When new people come into the company, they are told, at Microsoft, you are only as good as what you did in the last 5 minutes. No time to send trivia E-mail around the organisation, your 5 minutes is up."*

Last year, Bill earned £8 billion and he is now reputed to be the world's richest man. As this book goes to print, his net worth is reported to be $13.1 billion.

World class companies comprise just 2% of UK commerce so most of us figure somewhere in the remaining 98%. With a *"world class company"* like Microsoft, one has to ask oneself how right is he?

Is every member of your company working at peak efficiency and contribution? If not, you are losing money.

It is vital to run a job efficiently on a task basis, that is, asking the question on completion of every task, *"What is the next task I could meaningfully achieve, that will bring the maximum profit to my firm?"*

How many of us manage to run a job that way? If you did, you would be incredibly efficient in the use of your time, always thinking and acting towards being profitable.

I have only met one such person in the last twenty years who followed such a time-efficient way of working. He kept a book into which went notes of every phone call, in and out, every task to be achieved, time allowed for each task, notes on where things were filed and what happened to the work passed on to other managers.

He claimed it took no more than ten minutes each morning to organise priorities for that day, making up a hit list and leaving space for meetings and other occurrences. His company was getting the maximum out of that manager and certainly, he was the most efficient person I have ever met. He was easily able to relate to me the full details of a telephone conversation he had with a mutual colleague some eight months before.

What sort of company would you be running if all your employees achieved that discipline, examining priorities hourly?

- **IDEA:** Write down everything you intend to achieve in the week to come. As you complete each task, think about the most profitable thing you could do next. See how much more you achieve in the time and the extent of extra net profit you might make if you keep prioritising in this way.

- **IDEA:** List every job you have in your business and who is responsible for it. Against each task, estimate the length of time in hours or days it should take to complete properly and compare the schedule with your staffing levels. Is there anywhere you can increase efficiency or save time, and your biggest overhead cost - people?

*There is a great difference between being 'busy' and being 'effective'.*

**FULLY GUARANTEED**.

*Fully guaranteeing your work can result in your firm winning the business from a competitor. Sometimes, at marketing meetings, a principal will take twenty minutes discussing varying reasons why the company cannot commit itself to a full, refunding guarantee.*

Considered another way, what effect does one refund have on your annual turnover?  A satisfied customer will return to spend that refund over and over if treated correctly.  Ultimately you will benefit from their continued custom.

- **IDEA**:  If you have pride in what you do or supply, and in the systems and staff you have implemented, why not make a full guarantee the main stay of your mission statement?  It is very impressive.  The odd refund here or there to maintain good faith with a customer should not ruin you.  It will be very reassuring to the vast majority of reasonably-minded customers if you fully guarantee your product or service.

For example, Safeway promote pride in the freshness of their produce.  Recently, I went to a local store to return a cucumber with a blemish one might cut out.  Not only did I get a full refund after I was able to prove that it came from them, but in addition, I was given the choice of doubling the refund or having another cucumber as well.  That quality of service creates a good feeling towards that store over others.

The refund cost the store less than £2, while you might be dealing in hundreds or even thousands.  Given that the item probably only cost you about half what you charge your customer, how far are you able to extend a guarantee to instill complete confidence, to encourage your customers to buy from you repeatedly and with confidence?

Many guarantees are 'watered down' as Directors concern themselves with odd customers who might abuse the full guarantee.  The instances when this is likely are very few and only a full, '*no quibble*' guarantee reassures customers and enhances their decision to buy from you.  An example of this came from a restaurant in Fakenham who started off with a unique, innovative proposal - and then watered it down.  The back of their menu list read:

*"If you have difficulties in choosing the right menu, feel free to visit the kitchen for some guidance and sample some items (if available) before ordering."*

If the item you wish to try is not available, you wouldn't be able to sample it anyway so to say so, just waters down an otherwise superb guarantee idea.

At a seminar, I heard the story of the US store owner who positively attracted customer complaints as he considered it the best opportunity to gain their attention, answer their criticism and then sell to them.

If service means anything, dealing properly with objections is one way to demonstrate your concern that your customers do not feel disgruntled. Have you a firm customer relations policy in place?

- **IDEA**: Establish a complaints procedure so that one person in your organisation is trained in the procedure you wish to be followed, reporting *'incidents'* to management but also to the originating department for improvement. Publish the details centrally for all to see. That way, the same mistake does not happen twice as **all** employees are made fully aware of what happened.

**HELP HINT**: Always acknowledge any letter of complaint immediately even if there has not been time to look into the matter. If you are a customer, there is nothing more frustrating than the feeling that you are being ignored.

### SUMMARY

- Who handles complaints? It is better if just one person does it.

- Have you trained them in how to do it effectively so they know what you expect of them?

- Do you have a "*no quibble*" guarantee or have you diluted your guarantee to the extent that it really does not mean much?

## TRAINING

*Is one of your weaknesses the fact that you know every job in your business so well that you do not give enough thought to how well someone else might know it? Do you assume that they can 'pick it up'? Are you just 'too busy'? Under those circumstances, how can they give of their best unless you take the time and trouble to train them?*

### *No train, no gain!*

One of the businesses I admire most is based in the north of England. At any one time, this company has at least 10% of the workforce of 120 people on some kind of training course. This might consist of an internal work experience programme open to all levels or an Open University degree course. If *people are your greatest asset,* it is in your interest to pay for them to be trained, re-trained and trained again.

Business Link is a local company that can work with your local TEC and Chamber of Commerce providing training and help to all businesses small and large, shortly to include start-up's. Business advisors visit you to assess your needs and courses are subsidised with DTI grants.

Many Trade Associations provide industry qualifications which lead to certification in certain disciplines.

If your Trade Association does not offer such courses and examinations, then it is time the senior members met with the Trade Association or the TEC to develop some.

* **IDEA**: Why not talk to your local Business Link office, TEC, Chamber of Commerce or Trade Association about the training available to you and your staff.

### SUMMARY

* Look carefully at each member of staff and their work

* Do they have a job description; do they know what you want them to do, and how?

* Identify areas needing improvement and see if training is needed

* To get the most from each member of staff, motivate and train.

* Organise regular assessments so that progress can be monitored.

## ADVISORS

*There are a number of advisors you may consider using to bring an outside view to your business. The benefits can be considerable.*

Skills you might utilise are those of a marketing consultant, PR firm, database specialist, an advertising agency or creative design studio, the local Business Link advisor connected to the TEC or help from an accountant or bank. A computer freelance will be of great assistance in getting the most from your PC systems and is well worth recruiting to provide an advisory '*on call*' service.

Outsiders may seem expensive and unable to provide a **complete** answer to your problems. But they can provide considerable assistance in their discipline, helping you to stand back and see where things can be improved, make meaningful suggestions and so increase your business, training you to become more efficient with their skill.

The expense is well worthwhile for you will see the value of it year after year as you become more proficient. Learning how to maximise results from your promotional expenditure certainly can become an on-going skill. If as a prudent business person, you decide to appoint an advisor, you should set a budget and monitor expenses closely to ensure you get value from your commitment.

In this context, there is absolutely no doubt that you and your chosen advisor need to get on personally. It is a partnership you are creating. If you cannot work with your advisor find someone else. It is worth remembering that we are all different and we all have our own ways of doing things.

A fixed cost, marketing audit would be a positive first step, one which the author has constructed a special 'reader offer' around. You will find details on the last page. A marketing consultant should be able to conduct a professional SWOT analysis, provide a meaningful assessment of the business and produce a report to show you the areas to be attended to first and those longer term, together with a number of new ideas to increase profits. Costs of reports vary depending upon the size and nature of your business and the time taken. If the consultant is from some distance away, he or she will expect travel expenses.

In the longer term, you could decide to employ such a person to help you implement the plan and monitor it. This would be on an hourly rate or a retainer basis which will vary depending upon the hours you wish them to spend. An outsider brings a new view to the business. You may be too close to it.

The advisor's questions and ideas are valuable to you. If they haven't got any, they may not be right for your business. Experience counts. As an MD is speaking, outlining his thoughts and descriptions, an experienced marketing consultant or business advisor will be formulating ideas. The questions should be concerning what has been done, how well it was executed and whether it could be tried again.

Your advisor might not be an expert in your industry, although this has no bearing on their potential effectiveness to your business. Advisors cannot be expected to be highly knowledgeable in the technicalities of your industry or all those they work in. They will rely on you for that. Their skill is in their chosen discipline and they will bring new schemes and ideas from other industries.

You would be advised to run a six month trial for which you might be able to negotiate a lesser rate. When the person runs out of new ideas, it is time to move on. Often, a consultant might be willing to work on a job-for-job basis to cut back on costs for a small business. It is advisable for you to establish priorities and to outline a preliminary plan to be followed, whichever method you adopt.

**HELP HINT**:   If you decide to take on a marketing advisor, any promotional decisions that you take must be talked over first. It is pointless to allocate a budget to take on additional skills and then do something on your own initiative without consulting the advisor. *This practice often occurs.*

- **IDEA**:   Look in the Yellow Pages and select some consultants who could be of help to you. Choose one or two and see them for a preliminary discussion about ideas and costs. Always check whether the first appointment is without charge.

The best combination is teamwork, with you supplying the technical or product knowledge and the consultant injecting his expertise. How much do you really know about marketing? Reading this book may well bring you to the conclusion that it is all common sense. This is due to the way it has been written avoiding complicated text and definitions, but how many ideas suggested here have you implemented in the past?

The marketing consultant may be able to bring you other skills such as PR and most have associations with other promotional disciplines. A PR Consultant working for himself will be more dedicated to a smaller business and better value than a '*big PR firm*'. You can expect them to arrange a series of Press Releases and institute a press cutting service to record any press mentions. This provides a measure of their level of success since gaining press coverage for you is their skill.

A PR agent, should be able to raise awareness of your business but would not be expected to have much business development skill. Larger PR organisations have more sizeable overheads and so ask for larger retainer levels. Central London specialist PR firms will rarely take on a client for less than £3000 a month. It is better to find someone local.

**HELP HINT**:   Having another professional person thinking about your business can only be beneficial. With the advent of Business Link nationwide, a division of your local Training and Enterprise Council, grants, sometimes up to 50%, are available for various services including consultancy and training.

**HELP HINT**:   Subsidised training is one of the best services you can obtain from the TEC. Special development areas are well served by Government schemes. One call will put you on the mailing list and some useful, subsidised training courses are available covering sales, advertising, financial and marketing. Sometimes grants are available to produce publicity material but the schemes alter regularly and much depends on the location of your business.

## SITE SURVEYS

*Depending upon the trade you are in, another task a marketing consultant will achieve for you is a regular site survey.  You are probably much too close to the business to be able to achieve much from a walk round.*

You work in the premises every day.  In the pressure of day to day working, it is easy to forget, or not notice, the simple things that can enhance the site or bring attention to improving customer service where it is needed most.

By talking to your staff, listening to people doing their jobs in your business, an independent person, with a marketing or business development skill should be able to make worthwhile suggestions to benefit your business.  He or she will ask some pertinent questions and there will be considerable improvements obvious from a walk around the premises on a regular basis.

I remember a garden centre where I conducted a marketing audit, part of which was a site survey.  On the way out, past the tills as customers returned to their cars, they were greeted with a covered area which can only be described as a dumping ground.  It was full of cardboard boxes, old plant trays, a few odd bricks and various other paraphernalia.

In pointing this out, the client agreed that something should be done and they had been aware of it for some time but had not been able to think of a solution - so it was left as it was.  With some thought over a couple of months, they installed an exhibition display board showing the garden planning advice service available from this centre as well as a tasteful fountain set in a rockery with plants and small waterfalls.

The area is pleasant to look at and '*sells*' for that client where it had previously been a dumping ground, for over eighteen months.  It is easy to '*get used*' to such areas even though one is quite well aware that attention is needed.  With the passage of time, it becomes less and less noticeable to the people who work there every day, but an eye sore to customers.

## EMOTION

*Some will say it is obvious that being able to eliminate emotion from business decisions is an advantage. Even experienced people create needless, avoidable waste of net profit. Emotion can be useful in marketing but in some business dealings, it can kill profits.*

A recent discussion with a long-standing client persuaded me to include this section. It is too easy to '*think*' yourself into situations which then become real. Allowing emotion to control the situation colours your decision. I had gone to discuss a loyalty scheme proposal with this client who described the recent loss of a very large account caused by a change of contact. This account was important to the business representing a large profit element. The response to the question of its retrieval was surprising. *"We wouldn't bother"* the MD told me.

Apparently, the account was a large one which had been serviced for some years with a large measure of care which was appreciated by the buyer. When the buyer left, as happens often, his replacement brought in his own supplier and service deteriorated. The account was not an easy one to supply and deliveries suffered.

After eighteen months, pressure from that customer's staff demanded that a new supplier be found and the new buyer approached my client to ask if service could be resumed. My client refused. He felt that having been summarily dismissed after providing loyal and careful service for so long, *"they could jolly well find someone else"*.

This was not a sensible business decision. It was based purely on emotion and my client agreed on reflection that perhaps it was not very sensible for the furtherance of his business.

Some years ago, we supplied a black leaflet to a client having warned him that on folding, sometimes, black can crack and will not look perfect. He went ahead and sure enough, the black cracked. He refused to pay anything for the job and in discussion, the matter became a personal issue to him. Despite a number of meetings to try to find a solution, the client was adamant he would not pay and left us no choice than to sue him. The invoice total was £3500. He lost the case and his bill, with our costs, came to £18,000.

It should never have happened. His decision not to pay was based purely on emotion, not on good business acumen. Don't allow emotion to govern your business decisions even though it is the easiest thing to happen without you noticing.

Shortly after writing this page, I had a call from a client complaining about the front cover of his brochure. Although immaculate, his logo did just '*clip*' the photograph and it would have looked better without. Having prepared that for him in four days, I was angry that such a small point could even be mentioned when there was no time for a colour proof and the client was on holiday during production. I was advised by a friend to read my own book and bite my tongue.

# Chapter 5.
# PUTTING IT ALL TOGETHER

*The chances are your company is already using two or three of the marketing methods in this book. Every business person advertises something. But it is also likely that some of the techniques suggested you may never have used, or even contemplated. So how can you put all this information together? This chapter looks at how a small company grows bigger.*

## GETTING IT RIGHT

*It is possible that some readers will not choose to read this book from cover to cover. Instead, they may select subjects important to them to implement quickly. Thus, some of the best illustrative examples might be missed. This section lists some successful promotions used as examples featured in this book.*

1. **CONVERTING THE CHERRY PICKERS**.

   PAGE: 42  The promotion, so successful, it turned into a loyalty scheme.

2. **THE INNOVATIVE JANUARY SALE.**

   PAGE:45  A demonstration of the effective use of a combination of marketing methods.

3. **THE MAGNIFICENT MAILER**.

   PAGE: 75  An idea that seems to work in most industries.

4. **THE AUDIO PROMOTION WITH A SPECIAL PLUS.**

   PAGE: 85  A simple way to enhance a promotion which increased response.

5. **SEVEN DAY MADNESS**

   PAGE: 128 How to grab sales in the slow months

6. **GET PAID FASTER**

   PAGE: 131 Great idea for getting cash in quickly

7. **A PROSPEROUS DAY OUT.**

   PAGE: 151  How to sell to customers with larger requirements.

8. **CAN YOU CATCH YOUR LAPSED CUSTOMERS BEFORE THEY BECOME 'LOST'?**

   PAGE: 163  An immediate increase in sales.

A successful growing business will be run by someone innovative who is ahead of the game, not concerned in the least by competitors and who seizes every chance to exploit profit making opportunities. But even if that description does not fit you or your company, there are ways to capture more sales.

## INNOVATION - PART TWO

One way is to become more innovative. An innovative business is one which captures customers' attention by being different. Standing out from the crowd is what we spend our personal lives avoiding and our business lives encouraging. If your company carries on year after year doing the same old things, then to the customer, you are the same old company doing those same old things. If someone more energetic or interesting comes along, it might be time to change supplier.

The company with the more modern image, more sophisticated approach to service, more daring in promotion, is the one that will be noticed and attract business, as opposed to the one that consistently takes the safe or traditional route.

There is little to lose in planning something new, devoting some budget to testing the idea and then evaluating the response. Revamp it if it doesn't work and try again. A new strategy provides a source of motivation, especially if it works, while you may discover a way to obtain those additional sales.

There is nothing more successful or rewarding than promoting your company and product in a market where no one else in your industry is ever seen. Admittedly, those places are rare but nothing is impossible. If you get there first and the chap down the road is still complaining he is too busy to try something new, who wins?

## SUMMARY

- Follow through the planning stages in Chapter One. Look at the marketing methods and see what you are doing already.

- Make a note of ideas you did not think of and ways you might improve and work them into your marketing plan.

- Look at the other methods and understand them.

- Select one to try each month and do some testing.

- Make sure you have a marketing plan on your wall and note down promotional results.

## HOW A SMALL COMPANY GROWS BIGGER

*This is not a question that can be answered with a simple set of instructions because there are too many variables. However, you know that the success of your business is dependant on net profit. That is, profit **after** overheads and fixed costs, not gross profit and definitely not sales.*

At the beginning of this book, we said that the small business person is expected to be an expert in everything. Here, we look at the fundamental skills which take a growing business to the next level of trading.

### MANAGING CUSTOMER DEVELOPMENT

If customers are your lifeblood, then managing every customer to obtain the maximum it is possible for each to give you, in turn, produces the highest sales and profits.

The cost of attracting new customers is considerable in contrast to suggesting to people who already enjoy your good value, to buy more. Selling up is often forgotten in the maelstrom of daily tasks, yet the principle is established as a means to increase profits so easily. Customers who lapse can be attracted back if you know they have gone and rewarding people who continually contribute to your company success is an important factor.

One of the easiest ways to lose a customer over which you have little control is when your contact leaves. Whether through promotion or moving jobs, the contact you have nurtured sometimes for years leaves the buyer's role and a new person takes over. Invariably, the new buyer will want to use their own suppliers to ensure what to them is a more reliable service.

**IDEA**: There are two things you can do. First, wherever possible during a trading relationship, find excuses to communicate frequently with the buyer's immediate superior. A letter saying how helpful the buyer is always goes down well and there are always many other opportunities throughout a long-standing trading relationship. That way, if anything happens to move your contact, before the new man starts, you can be in the superior's office guaranteeing continuity, personal handling of their account in the interim and free product training to the new man.

**IDEA**: The second method might be useful where the first has been difficult. When the new person starts, be nice, be understanding, ensure they know you are always there in case of difficulties - and wait. Often, the new service is not as good as the old and the staff will ask for you to resume as supplier. Sometimes, the new supplier truly is not as good and you can help out *'in emergencies'*. By always being there, not allowing emotion into the equation and showing perfect service and good value, the chances are it will not be long before you are called upon again to supply the whole order.

### MANAGING GROWTH

As you trade, year after year, you become more proficient at building the customer base. If you are careful with cash, you will have reserves to use, to fund serving customers who have larger spending requirements than those you have served up to now. National companies are made up of people and although better trained and more professional, a buying decision rests with one, or just a few of those people.

Bigger orders mean a greater strain on your capabilities so the foundation needs to be strong, but given the right conditions, most principals can make the successful transition to increasing through-put. With the right financing, staff, service and attitude, a confident approach can win big business.

### MANAGING TIME

I once heard a defendant being sued in Court, say to his star witness at the end of the case, *'Chris, I think we have been busy fools'*. This was not so much because they lost the case, but rather that in losing, the realisation had dawned on him that being *busy* does not necessarily mean being *profitable*.

In the section on the use of time, I quoted Bill Gates' comments on efficiency. It goes without saying that the manager who consistently reviews his priorities after every task is likely to be generating as much profit as he can.

But profit is more than time management. It involves buying properly, obtaining three quotes minimum on everything, preferably more, and never taking *'no'* for an answer. These days, an estimate is only the cost of a fax. It means keeping suppliers happy, getting the most from them, and once in a while, checking costs to keep them as tight as possible.

### MANAGING EMPLOYEES

Staff are often the greatest cost to your business. You know how expensive they are to run, that they do not do it your way, and it takes more of your time to supervise them correctly.

Selection, training and control are paramount towards maximising the contribution from every member of staff as they can be your greatest asset. Make sure employees have a proper job specification so that they know what you expect of them. Conduct frequent job appraisals, however small your business. Involve them in decisions so that they know what you are planning and why. That way, you create and motivate a team.

Above all, be ruthless when someone has ceased to make a useful contribution, and act quickly. People do "wear out" and get stale, but they also find an unsatisfactory job lacks challenge in their lives, providing no satisfaction of a good day's work being done.

You have a responsibility to your employees to provide them with a fulfilling job and the training and help they need. But if an employee is not making a contribution then the business must come first.

Nobody enjoys a termination interview and these days, you have to be very careful how you go about it, so make sure you understand what the Law requires. Your local Job Centre has booklets if you are uncertain of correct procedure. Usually, it is better for everyone, including the employee, to take the decision and bite the bullet.

## Managing Cashflow

Cashflow ineptitude is the cause of many business failures because running a growing business with time constraints and task variations means that there is little time to watch the finances. If the sales graph moves upwards, you can be lulled into thinking everything is going in the right direction, when in fact, the opposite might be the case. Sales levels do not take account of costs and can confuse the issue of a company's success or failure.

If the people who owe you money are holding on to it, your sales mean nothing. If you have to borrow the funds to keep going, your costs are higher than they need be. If a new piece of software or machinery looks attractive, can you purchase that out of liquid funds or will you need to borrow?

Often, it is better to avoid the additional cost of borrowing, particularly with interest rates rising to combat inflation.

It could be argued that small business finance is not a marketing matter. However, the basic marketing principles of good communication and repetition can apply to extracting your rightly due payment in the same way they help to create a proper sales environment.

The initial reaction is to '*threaten*' and some business people do not realise that as well as being against the Law, it is not a sensible way to go about matters. You must retain the business.

### *A sale is not a sale until the money's in the Bank.*

One way to help the financial position is to develop Terms of Trading, and stick to them rigidly. One clause should deal with late payment stipulating that interest will be charged on the whole sum from the date of invoice if it is not paid on time. The interest rate I use is 8%, the same as that in The County Court if matters ever need to get that far. By issuing an '*interest invoice*' a debtor is encouraged to produce a cheque for the sum owed to save paying the interest. In practice, the resulting payment may not include the interest element which is an encouragement to pay rather than a source of net profit. Sometimes, even the threat of interest can be enough to produce a payment. Remember, VAT can not be charged on '*interest*'.

It is a constant complaint of small business that large companies keep them waiting for payment. This can be avoided by taking the right steps when you agree the terms of the contract which can be achieved by exchanging letters, to constitute an '*offer*' and an '*acceptance*', the basis of all contracts. Make sure any agreement is confirmed in writing and that the period in which you expect to be paid is clear. This does not have to be 30 days. You might choose to render a seven or fourteen day invoice, especially on new accounts. There is no harm in allowing no credit at all until your new customer has proved his good will providing your reasons are clearly explained to your customer and accepted. It does take time to set up a credit account if you conduct a company search and take out trade references. During that period, you should not provide credit anyway and there is no reason why this policy should lose you any business.

Credit control may be another case of *"We've always done it like that"* and that is no reason to continue with an outdated policy.

All prospects who place an order should be checked with a search at Company's House to ascertain their position. By fax, that costs around £20 and is a sensible investment. If matters do turn sour, those sheets contain the names and home addresses of all the Directors and a letter to a Director's home where their partner may see it can have a dramatic effect in prompting payment.

Spend some time at The County Court, or read their booklets to learn the simple procedure. With debtors who are also small businesses, a summons which you can prepare and submit without a solicitor can often be enough to produce a payment. You can search the records of Judgement for the name of any potential customer or supplier to make sure there are no judgements outstanding against them before you trade.

There is no doubt that an outstanding Judgement can affect the ease or difficulty with which they can gain credit. If a Judgement is made against you while you are working at your home address, the credit rating of all the residents living there can be affected.

Some companies are able to increase their prices slightly to allow a margin for an '*early payment discount*'. Invariably, these options are taken up by the customer. I know of one company who eliminated their overdraft overnight by implementing that suggestion.

There is a fine line to draw between '*getting paid*' and retaining customer goodwill for future business which can only be a matter for your judgement as there are no hard and fast rules. However, it is easy to let emotion rule decisions when matters are so obviously unjust and it is then that wrong decisions might be made. There is no room for emotion in business.

Financial prudence is a skill every small business person can develop. So is the ability to negotiate, never to give in on your price, not agreeing to someone's first or even third offer, and to be *"in tune"* with your company's financial position, in detail, every minute of the day.

There are thousands of companies who go to the wall with bulging order books. These are the ones who lost sight of net profit and concentrated on sales or turnover. It does not follow that because your sales increase, your net profit increases. It is added costs that are so ruinous to any medium or long term plan. It is easy to order a new computer, even a Porsche, just because the cash happens to be there. Next month, it might not be and you will have a problem if you made an impulse purchase.

Cash management, cashflow manipulation, long term strategic planning, all are important if one day, you want to be publicly quoted or become a big player in your industry. If your products are in demand, of good quality and sensibly priced, your market is established, financial planning in place and under control and marketing and promotions giving you profitable growth, there is absolutely no reason why you should not, in time, be amongst the UK's 2% world class companies.

## CONSIDER THE FUTURE AND PLAN

If you do have your business under control, start planning to take on larger customers with greater requirements. Plan ahead using your resources so you are able to make an effective presentation to a really large prospect. Obviously, if you are working out of the back of a garage, you will need to move to smarter premises to impress your visitors or meet them in a hotel. You will need to think carefully about how much budget to put aside, to plan and prepare a new set of publicity material, brochures and product leaflets.

Larger amounts of business have to be funded for longer periods. There may be a greater amount of raw material needed if you manufacture or a bigger supplier's cost if a larger order is imported. Those suppliers will need paying within their normal periods, often before your customer pays you and that has to be funded together with any higher cost of borrowing.

Once you have consolidated your position and you have some funds to move forward, now is the time to plan for growth. Who will you target, what will be their needs, how will you answer the objections which you will encounter, and overall, what is the most effective way to approach them?

If your prospect is a national company, they are run by people. They are professional in their dealings with smaller companies, courteous and informative and there is no reason whatever why you should not approach them. Start the research process by evaluating how you could be become a supplier.

As long as your product meets the specification, a new prospect will need total assurance of your capability rather than *how* you do what you do. It is important to realise just how difficult it is for your prospect to abandon their present supplier in favour of your company, an unknown quantity until tested. This is why it might be easier to secure a trial order, to *prove* your service. All you need to secure larger orders is a well planned approach and a little luck.

# THE ART OF THE MARKETING MIX

*Throughout the book, various marketing methods have been examined as single activities. It is now time to consider running different campaigns at the same time.*

In order to demonstrate the way any business can promote products or services constantly, let us use the example of selling of a book on marketing.

As with many small business promotions, there is a limited budget. It would be better to sell direct to end users rather than through bookshops, to maximise the available profit. Remember the power of the word 'direct'. What methods could be used at low cost to sell copies to as many end users as possible?

1.  TESTIMONIALS

Any book needs a well designed cover, a good, descriptive name and testimonials from notable people to give it credence. A good marketing idea is a Union Jack to show the book is **for** British people, **by** British people.

2.  SHARED MAILINGS

Using the idea of shared mailings, the first contacts could come from anyone seeking to reach the same market as ours.

3.  SPONSORS

Large company sponsors could use the book as a *'giveaway'* incentive to customers in order to reward loyalty or attract new ones.

4.  NETWORKING

Invitations to speak at gatherings of small business people can be a golden chance to sell books. This adds credibility to your standing as people who give instructional talks are generally perceived as experts in their field.

5.  READER OFFERS.

This is where a paper or periodical features a review of the book and then offers it to readers at a discount. This method reaches the heart of the target market.

6.    ARTICLES

Writing in National Trade magazines, using the book as a source, sells more books.

7.    FAXSHOTS

There is some distaste for using the fax for selling but the method is worth a trial of 2000 faxshots to small companies.

8.    LATERAL MARKETING

If a marketing book is written especially to be easily understood, there may be other markets. Schools have sixth form economics and business studies classes - a lateral market. That would best be reached by mailing using a list from a schools list specialist.

9.    MAIL ORDER

Mail order companies who specialise in selling books to small businesses by mail may take the book to add to their range. This reaches the target market directly.

10.    MAILINGS

'Go direct' to growing businesses by selecting a list and send a mailing.

11.    COMMERCIAL POINT OF SALE

Consider what might be included with the book to reach the actual buyer. One example might include a voucher with a discount off another copy as a Christmas gift for a business colleague. That sale cost nothing.

12.    THE INTERNET

The audience on the Internet is global.  It is possible to reach millions of potential buyers this way. The key to success is the search words.

13.    ADVERTISING

Most businesses think of advertising as the easiest marketing method but it can be the most wasteful. In this case, we are looking to target directly, so advertising may be ineffective. We need to test.

14.    PUBLIC RELATIONS

An effective use of PR would be sending a book to be reviewed but Press Releases to selected journals might increase awareness.

15.    SEMINARS

By mounting seminars based on the book content, revenue will be produced as well as sales of the book to delegates as course notes.

16.    EXHIBITIONS

We need to be able to show the book to as many people as possible but for a low cost.  One way might be to select an exhibition and ask the organiser if there is an exhibitor who might be willing to share a stand.

This could be a very good way to sell a large number of books quickly.  It is a face-to-face selling situation and providing you take enough stock, buyers can purchase on the spot.

**Summary**

*   There is no doubt that significant growth can result from combining various marketing methods, controlling them all properly, monitoring and refining.

*   This list of marketing methods could be doubled. Combining traditional and innovative methods running side by side could be very successful. This is the sort of thinking that all businesses need to construct when they refine their marketing plan.

## SHOULD YOU STILL 'MARKET' WHEN ALL IS WELL?

Recently, I was asked to speak at a business breakfast meeting where I sat next to the proprietor of a very profitable business who installed swimming pools. We were discussing how the discipline of marketing should affect him now that he had built a successful, profitable business. The conversation raised an important point.

What he wanted to know was, how should his marketing be directed now things were running well? Surely there was no need to promote all the time?

In talking, it was intriguing to hear that as with many businesses, he had never decided what his aims were. He had no idea or plan to lead him to his goal. Business planning was covered in our early chapters as something that is vital to success. He could have opened a new branch in another area, recruited a manager to take over his very successful business so he could semi-retire, or generate income for investment. There was simply no plan, it had all *'just happened'*.

With a full order book and good margins, you can begin to look at all orders that come in to ensure that each produces not just a good margin, but an excellent one. In simple terms, you could process less work for a higher return. This could involve a price increase. If you are successfully supplying a market which is accepting your prices, there may be room to increase them without too much reduction in demand, even when your margins are already good. Clearly, if you can transact less business and make a higher return, you should. As usual, it is down to careful testing.

- **IDEA**: You might like to look at creating what I will call *'pension products'*. That is *'after sales'* products or services needed by the consumer that go on and on. This is very good business and the reason why so many *'maintenance'* firms do so well.

When the order book is full, the margins are good and you are comfortable, it is not the time to relax the marketing. The common-sense position is that none of us know what's round the corner. A fire in my building had a catastrophic effect on my annual income. So promoting all the time, even when business is good, is vital.

**CAUTION**: One thing to watch. If you receive an order you do not really want, do not point prospects to a competing business. It is far better to say that you can not fulfill the order for six months so as to delay the order, rather than pass it directly to a competitor which will help him compete with you and perhaps become stronger in the future. Even when things are running well, marketing **is** a critical discipline in your business.

## Chapter 6
## FUTURE MARKETING

*Part of the marketing brief is to be aware of new ideas and keep up with new ways of selling. This section examines some approaches set to become part of the future of marketing. None are outrageous, some are a couple of years away, but they are noted here to remind you to be aware of new ideas. If you don't, your competitors will*

- The Internet - should a small business be there?

- The Weather - a reliable prediction service up to eleven months ahead for weather-dependant businesses, available now

- Information Technology - how it affects us, a way of producing dynamic point of sale

- Virtual Reality - the way everything will be designed in eighteen months time

- Mondex - the cashless society, and not only in retailing

# THE INTERNET

It is a difficult decision for a small company to decide on the '*worth*' of a presence on the Internet. The Internet is an excellent example of a facility designed for one purpose being put to another. The academics who developed it to exchange information could never have realised that their facility would be connected to over 30% of the world's households within the first 10 years. After all, that was not the original purpose.

There is no doubt that business communication will eventually demand the use of an E-Mail facility, an unrivaled advantage of being connected to the Internet. The computer industry is now looking at making the network of file servers, which make up the Internet, more reliable and faster.

Transacting business via the Internet is another matter and still in it's infancy. Some believe the Internet cannot assist business and shows no potential whatever. In fact, Argos stores recently took space on the virtual shopping mall, Barclay Square, a web site sponsored by Barclays Bank. In the last 9 months, Argos has notched up a mere 22 sales. A report commissioned by Healey and Baker recently surveyed British shoppers and revealed that although a massive £7.25 billion of annual consumer spending in the UK could be diverted to electronic retailing over the next few years, only 20% of the 2000 adults interviewed in the survey said that they were interested in using electronic shopping and just 0.3% claimed to shop electronically at present. So progress is slow.

Yet, more and more private individuals are linking their home computers to the Internet, or information super highway, and browsing through pages selling many different products. At least 20% of new Internet sites established each year are from businesses. Even moving sales presentations can be placed on your page.

Establishing an Internet page for your business costs around £400 and may be a worthwhile investment as the medium grows and develops. The cost to establish an Internet page is minimal against other forms of promotion and only you can judge when to place your company ahead of your competitors in this way.

Even today, were you sitting in an aircraft with your laptop computer turned on, you could connect to the Internet while cruising 30,000 feet up and be able to communicate with anyone sitting on the opposite side of the world, or keeping in touch with your business.

Whether we like it or not, we are entering a new age of commerce as people begin to enjoy an element of shopping from home and the applications for smaller businesses are numerous so it is worth spending time to keep track of developments. If the whole thing is a mystery, pay a visit to the Cyber Cafe in London where coffee drinkers can indulge in self-education by 'surfing the net'.

## THE WEATHER

There is little need to ask anyone connected with business how important the weather can be to their delivery schedules. Recently, Garden Centre groups have run trials, with The Met Office predicting weather patterns at weekends, in order to save vast stocks of outdoor plants from frost, strong winds and the odd hurricane, to say nothing of arranging staffing levels more cost effectively.

Almost all commercial organisations can benefit from knowing how the weather will effect their delivery schedule, and hence, their customer service. Delivery of perishable goods is another application.

The trial service with The Met Office, gives a five day forecast and costs around £60 per week. It is called the Weather Initiative and arrives via the fax machine. Predictions become less reliable towards the end of the five days but as a guide to the required staffing levels and the effects on business, it far surpasses strolling outside and raising a licked index finger.

The future lies with a new service which uses research conducted at the University of South London, called Weather Action. Specialising in long range forecasting which the Met Office admits it cannot match, Weather Action provides a full forecast on all local or national weather factors in the medium term up to thirty days, and in the long range **up to eleven months ahead**. The medium term forecast comes as a four page bulletin for each of the thirty days including information on rainfall, temperature, air activity and sunshine, with easy-to-read charts and information providing accuracy levels for the previous months. They even offer special ski weather information numbers for the following season. The subscription is presently £5 per week. The service can be accessed by fax or by telephone.

This method boasts an 80% accuracy rate, the same as the Met Office and is considerably cheaper. It is a service the Met Office admits it cannot provide, especially in terms of long range weather forecasting up to eleven months ahead. The Met Office is perfectly happy to supply five days ahead and will reluctantly go to thirty days if pushed. Weather Action relies solely on the interpretation of sun spot activity rather than computer modules of synoptic conditions and historical information.

Weather Action base their forecasts on a method called Solar Weather Technique. Research is continuing to improve the quality of the forecast. Scientists in the programme predict that within a year or two, they will be accurately predicting weather 2 - 5 years ahead. Already, their results are impressive. How would an 80% accuracy rate affect your business?

## IT FOR TRAINING.

With the technology explosion seen in recent years, imagine how far this could affect the way you sell to your customers only limited by the scope of your imagination and the power of your PC. In training terms, it could already save hours.

The touch screen information computer, already in existence, seems under-used in business. Perhaps few customers or potential customers visit a commercial supplier.

However, staff training has benefited greatly from this technology. A US company, Applied Learning, installs touch screen computers in a work room close to the staff canteen, loaded with learning software. When members of staff take a break, they go to the special area, sit at a screen and enter a password. The computer recognises them and leads them back to the place where they previously left off.

The programme can teach, test, and if necessary return to the original lesson. At the log off, it produces a report on how progress is going and where weaknesses lie. Firms installing the computers find staff quite willing to increase skills in this way and to use their spare time to further their knowledge.

### VIRTUAL REALITY

The step beyond computer CD's is virtual reality. Although some readers might feel VR is extreme, all design companies will be using it soon. As technology advances and helmet size and weight decrease, or disappear, what futuristic applications could be found for such a tool?

Designers of all types are very quickly understanding the advantages of being able instantly to see the effect of a change. Our eyes take in visual 3D images far faster than text.

Your customer will be able to plan his new office with all his furnishings available from you. By selecting 'yes', 'no' or 'options' on a control panel in front of a screen, he will see it appear before him in full colour and in 3D allowing the full effect of a change of mind to be assessed instantly.

By entering the size of the floor area, the computer calculates exactly the quantities of materials needed. On the screen, you see the office, in 3-D and so have the chance to alter things around to be more efficient. This leads to an order form from the printer that even shows the quickest route for the deliveries to the customer, and the day and time of delivery.

Another application might be for customers of a garden centre to enter a list of parameters specific to their garden: size, facing direction, type of soil and so on, and then be told of a range of plants suitable by colour, grouping, and price range.

A print out with the garden centre's name is sent to the customer and is looked at by friends and other family members. What could be sold to a customer who accesses a simple, what-to-do-in-the-garden video CD? What a good PR opportunity.

What better way to fill your garden with plants than to select them, see them grow before you, and then order them. It really does not take much imagination to think of other applications - selecting wallpaper: *'there's your room, done in different styles'*. The fashion industry where you can show how it will look on the customer.

The savings in design terms are immense and it is in this area that great developments are taking place. VR in the commercial world is superseding its use as a games player. The planning of a garden is already in use. The software costs about £30 and runs on almost any PC.

## MONDEX

Can we dispense with cash? If the Mondex trial in Swindon is anything to go by, probably not. Mondex is an electronic cashless system devised by Nat West, BT and the Midland. Of Swindon's population of 190,000, just 9,000 people have opted for the card from a target of 40,000, even though the test scheme is free.

The indications are that results may be positive when people change their habits and accept the use of plastic debit cards instead of cash but full customer acceptance is still some way off.

Electronic data transfer is with us and many commercial organisations are seeing the benefits to be gained from product group selection, stock searching, ordering and paying on line. In marketing terms, this is a beneficial method for a commercial organisation as customers using EDI are likely to remain loyal.

Many businesses believe electronic trading is not secure and that too much can go wrong. In the early days that may have been so, with people ordering goods from the other side of the world through the Internet, but today with advanced encryption devices, it will become a much safer way to transact.

## CONCLUSION

- Running a business on a daily basis means long hours, hard work, sometimes six or even seven days a week. You have absolute responsibility for your own future and that of your staff. You are beset with advice from all quarters, can you take a rational decision during the daily round? Use the information here to help.

- There is no point in giving up on marketing, either because you are a growing business or know nothing about it. You have an advantage over big business in being able to respond and react quickly without the need for numerous meetings. Be pro-active - all the time.

- Plan, execute, monitor, adjust, repeat, monitor, adjust, test, monitor, plan...

- Make decisions only you can make, about how you want to run your business and how you wish it to be perceived. Take the time. It will pay for itself in the long run.

- There are twenty three marketing methods in this book to help you to decide how to proceed. If you want to learn about them in depth, go on a course. **No train, no gain**. Business seminars are good for lots of reasons. They inform, motivate, encourage and nudge you in the right direction.

- Use networking as much as you can. It can lead to lots of opportunities for very little outlay.

- Have one eye on the present and the other on the future. Remember, your competitor is watching you. Get ahead and stay there.

- Attend to the customers you have. They took blood and sweat to acquire, do not let them drift away because you really can't be bothered with them. They pay the bills, they support all your aspirations. Look after them and make sure you never let one down.

- Efficient use of time for testing is paramount in running a successful business or promotion. If you do not plan it, you lose response. If you lose response, you lose what you are there for net profit.

- Chase net profit, not sales. Never give in to a request for a lower price without a lowering in specification or service. Leave some leeway in negotiations. Always start higher than you need as it is surprising how many will still say *"yes"*. Never drop on price.

- Sometimes, positive results to overall profitability, come from marketing methods which are chosen to be specific to that business at that time. The secret is in targeting as finely and imaginatively as you can.

- Every customer you attract and keep buys from you, not your competitor. The benefit they give you will go on and on if you look after them.

- The customer is **always** right - **always**. Even when they're wrong, they're right. To give one refund will make them loyal to you and what is a small loss in comparison to your year's turnover? One happy customer tells others. So does an unhappy customer, who, according to one survey, tells 27 others on average.

- You can implement a marketing programme which will show you a good return if conducted properly, however *"small"* your business is. To that end, good luck!


**"A journey of a thousand miles**

**starts with a single step...."**


*Mao Tse Tung.*


**THE END**

## APPENDIX

**THE FOLLOWING SELF-HELP FORMS ARE IN ORDER:**

1.      *SWOT Analysis*; the starting point in self-assessment to put on paper what you **think** you know about your business.  This form is only intended as a starting point, you must add what you need to know about your business.  Conducted regularly, this will be invaluable as a document to steer your business by.

2.      ***Formulate a marketing plan***; designed to start you towards thinking along the correct lines to give you a plan of promotional activity, set out for the year. It should serve as a measure of success to decide on future activity.

3.      ***Advertising media***; a starting point in evaluating the media.  It introduces you to the cost per 1000 method of comparing various media and gauging success by evaluating the cost of each response.  Work with the form as a basis and add your own formula to personalise your results. Repetition sells, repetition sells, repetition sells.

4.      *A **short advertisement audit***; are you getting the most from your advertising?  This sheet asks you the basic questions before you go further into the advertising section.

5.      ***The Fundamentals***; this section is a starting point in answering the two basic problem areas most companies complain of - not enough customers, or those who come not spending enough.  The chances are you will never be satisfied with either figure but this list starts you off and you can add local ideas to it.  It serves as a training and motivation subject for your next staff meeting.  What ideas do they have?

6.      ***Short Questionnaire***; this form gives a '*snapshot*' of your situation on which to base other ideas. Use this sheet as a basis and once having identified what you think your problems are, ask your public about your business.

7.      ***How to brief a graphic design studio***; this is a check list of things you need to think about before the designer arrives.

| 1st - 6 MONTHS | SWOT ANALYSIS<br><br>2nd - 6 MONTHS | POINTS TO CONSIDER |
|---|---|---|
| **STRENGTHS** | | - Customer care<br>- Staff performance<br>- Cash reserves<br>- Customer flow<br>- POS<br>- Loyalty scheme<br>- Premises<br>- Layout<br>- Product mix<br>- New markets<br>- Competition<br>- Cashflow<br>- Promotional planning<br>- The premises<br>- Manufacturer contact<br>- Incoming phone calls<br>- Delivery<br>- Sourcing<br>- Van fleet<br>- Promotional experience<br>- Quality control<br>- Capital equipment<br>- Management - Technique<br>             Training<br>             Supervisors |
| **WEAKNESSES** | | |
| **OPPORTUNITIES** | | - Suppliers<br>- Competitors<br>- R & D<br>- Product development<br>- Sickness record<br>- Historical<br>- Market<br>- Awareness<br>- PR<br>- Local Press<br>- Trade Press<br>- Telesales<br>- Representation<br>- Use of time<br>- General efficiency<br>- Customer perception<br>- Timekeeping<br>- Methods<br>- Admin<br>- Purchasing |
| **THREATS** | | |
| **NOTES ON ACTION** | | |

# FORMULATE A MARKETING PLAN

| MONTH | | WHAT WE DID LAST YEAR (Major & minor promotions) | ✓ If repeat-ing | | NEW PROMOTIONS PLANNED THIS YEAR | Estimate cost actual | Attributable profit estimate | Change from last year + / - |
|---|---|---|---|---|---|---|---|---|
| JAN | 1 2 3 4 | | | 1 2 3 4 | | | | |
| FEB | 1 2 3 4 | | | 1 2 3 4 | | | | |
| MAR | 1 2 3 4 | | | 1 2 3 4 | | | | |
| APR | 1 2 3 4 | | | 1 2 3 4 | | | | |
| MAY | 1 2 3 4 | | | 1 2 3 4 | | | | |
| JUNE | 1 2 3 4 | | | 1 2 3 4 | | | | |
| JULY | 1 2 3 4 | | | 1 2 3 4 | | | | |
| AUGUST | 1 2 3 4 | | | 1 2 3 4 | | | | |

| MONTH | | WHAT WE DID LAST YEAR (Major & minor promotions) | ✓ If repeat-ing | | NEW PROMOTIONS PLANNED THIS YEAR | Estimate cost actual | Attributable profit estimate | Change from last year + / - |
|---|---|---|---|---|---|---|---|---|
| S E P T | 1 2 3 4 | | | 1 2 3 4 | | | | |
| O C T | 1 2 3 4 | | | 1 2 3 4 | | | | |
| N O V | 1 2 3 4 | | | 1 2 3 4 | | | | |
| D E C | 1 2 3 4 | | | 1 2 3 4 | | | | |

As you complete a promotion or campaign, write up the details and then enter it into the same month, 12 months on. That way, your plan is constantly being updated and refined and your decisions are based on results rather than 'gut feel'.

As you become more experienced, try to vary the periods of the campaign so that they are not predictable and customers see variation from time to time.

### *Innovation captures the imagination and becomes memorable*

| | LIST ALL MEDIA USED LAST YEAR | ❶ CIRCULATION (IN 1,000'S TO NEAREST 1,000) | ❷ COST PER INSERTION | COST PER 1,000 DIVIDE ❷ BY❶ | ❸ ACTUAL No. OF RESPONSES | COST PER RESPONSE ❷ x No OF INSERTIONS ÷ ❸ |
|---|---|---|---|---|---|---|
| 1 | | | | | | |
| 2 | | | | | | |
| 3 | | | | | | |
| 4 | | | | | | |
| 5 | | | | | | |
| 6 | | | | | | |
| 7 | | | | | | |
| 8 | | | | | | |

**ADVERTISING MEDIA**

## LIST AGAIN IN ORDER OF RESPONSES EACH WEEK

| WK | 1 | 2 | 3 | 4 | 5 | 6 | 7 | 8 | 9 | 10 | 11 | 12 | 13 | 14 | 15 | 16 | 17 | 18 |
|---|---|---|---|---|---|---|---|---|---|---|---|---|---|---|---|---|---|---|
| 1 | | | | | | | | | | | | | | | | | | |
| 2 | | | | | | | | | | | | | | | | | | |
| 3 | | | | | | | | | | | | | | | | | | |
| 4 | | | | | | | | | | | | | | | | | | |
| 5 | | | | | | | | | | | | | | | | | | |
| 6 | | | | | | | | | | | | | | | | | | |
| 7 | | | | | | | | | | | | | | | | | | |

Use this template to cover the 52 weeks in the year rather than just eighteen as shown here.

**TAKE A COPY OF THE PAGE CONTAINING YOUR TRADE ADVERTISEMENT.**

1. Does your advertisement stand out on the page? Has it an attention seeking headline using the right words? Is the headline clear or confusing (ask a customer for comments).

2. Does it attract attention? Are you listing USP's? Is there too much text, could you use bullet points?

3. Does your advertisement say, *"Here we are"* or does it have an element of, *"Contact us now and send for (an offer)"* so that you can measure response?

4. How many responses each period *(weekly, monthly)* do you get? Use the advertisement response form in the appendix pages to find out.

5. How does it compare with competitors, better/worse? Does their advertisement stand out? What are they doing that you are not?

6. If their advertisement is better than yours, why? Is it style, content, layout, offer? What is 'weak' about their advertisement?

7. List what they provide and check yours against the list. What can you offer that your competitors don't?

8. Do you have a 'positioning statement' /strapline?

9. Is there a clear *'call to action'*? Do people who reply appreciate what you want them to do?

10. Are you buying well enough ie: regular insertion rate? When did you last negotiate? Can you *'spot place'*? Can you *'lodge' bromides*?

11. Have you called the magazine to see if you could provide reader offers, or write a column about your industry?

# THE FUNDAMENTALS

## WHAT IS YOUR PROBLEM?

*Not enough customers*, in which case:

- Questionnaire, where are they coming from?
- Advertisements in Trade Press with coupons to send in for 'details', or vouchers off a purchase. What could you offer them?
- Mailings to the locality, Post Office leaflet drops to post coded areas.
- Special promotions to attract new customers to open evenings, 10% OFF evenings, lectures and tours.
- Liaison with local organisations to share lists for mailing or joint mailings.
- Joint promotions with other local non-competing businesses
- Join the Chamber of Commerce networking lunches
- Think of other marketing methods, tele-sales, newsletter etc.

OR

*The customers we have do not spend enough*

- Loyalty scheme needed now!
- "£1 voucher for every £20 spent" type of approach.
- Customer questionnaire to give you more knowledge of what they want.
- Promotions to inform them of your whole range, less known products as well as necessities.
- Selling up philosophy needed
- Lively signage with suggestions to purchase, leaflets in deliveries on special offer products.
- Spread the product range, link products in groups purchasable together.
- Check if staff are 'selling' or 'helping'?
- Two-for-the-price-of-one promotions to 'stack out' on selected everyday products.
- Red spot promotions in your catalogue (everything with a red spot 10% off this month).

# QUESTIONNAIRE

NAME......................................................................................................................................

COMPANY.............................................................................................................................

ADDRESS...............................................................................................................................

....................................................................................................................................................

POSTCODE.............................................................

How many times have you used our company before: (Please circle)

        1st time            2-5            6-10            Lots

How many times have you used a service like ours this year: (Please circle)

      Not many            Now & Then            Lots

Who else do you use to supply you with similar product and what % of your business do they get?

1.                        %

2.                        %

3.                        %

What product ranges do you expect us to stock here?

.......................................................................................................................................

Can you always obtain what you need from us?                YES / NO

Last time you ordered, did you buy more than you intended to?      YES / NO

How do you rate us for the following: (Please ✓ box as applicable) PLEASE BE FRANK!

| | Excellent | Good | Satisfactory | Poor |
|---|---|---|---|---|
| Overall presentation: Catalogue can you find what you want easily? | | | | |
| Product range: Did we stock what you needed? | | | | |
| Staff knowledge when you call us? | | | | |
| How would you rate our delivery service? | | | | |
| Service: How have our staff treated you? | | | | |

Would you use us more often if we provided a loyalty scheme?.......................................................

Which Trade paper do you read?

*Thank you for your time.*

# DESIGN STUDIO JOB BRIEF

**JOB:**....................
....................................................................**NAME:**........................................................
...................................**JOB NUMBER**:......................................
What is the item: Brochure, Advertisement, Flyer, Mailer, Exhibition stand or graphics?

**DESCRIBE:**................

Who is it designed to reach?

What sort of people are they?

What will appeal to those people?

What sort of approach should we seek, modern and trendy/more conservative?

Do you want lots of colour and excitement or a very professional approach?

Are there any points we must know about those people you wish us to portray?

How will the item be used?

Describe the product or service you wish to feature in detail?

What are the sales points you wish to bring out or feature, in order of importance?

What result are you looking for?

How do you want prospects to respond to you?

**ORIGINATION** to be used on other items as follows:

Extent: (No of pages)?

Material covers: Weight of paper and type, say 300gsm, white art board?

Material inside : Weight of paper and type, say 175 gsm, matt coated or gloss art?

Number of colours, covers?

Number of colours inside?

**FINISHING**:

UV spot gloss varnish covers

Matt or Gloss Lamination

Saddle stitch, spiral bound, perfect bound.

**DATES REQUIRED**:

Delivery:

Quotation:

Visuals:                              Deliver to:

*Don't miss this chance for Hands-On Help.....*

# 25% off a full, marketing audit.

Offer only available to registered readers of "Hands-On Marketing."
Valid for 60 days after purchase.

The author of this book, Colin Rees is providing a full 25% off the current fee to conduct a half-day, full marketing audit on your premises.

This means that for just £300 + travel + vat, your company can be provided with the full experience and knowledge that has gone into the writing of this book and have that experience applied specifically to **your** business. There are no extras the cost is all-inclusive.

The audit includes a SWOT analysis, ideas and suggestions to expand your business, make it more profitable, and help with deciding positioning or USP's. A full, written report follows each visit. It is an excellent opportunity for you to ask for any additional information or explanation you wish from the book content.

To make an appointment, call Quest Consultants Ltd on **01992 500 530**, or write to: Quest, Freepost, SG 444, Hertford, SG14 1YA.

*Dear Reader,*
*Thank you for buying this book. I hope it has been, or will be of use to you in running your business and improving your profits. Please feel free to call me if you need any explanation. My "Hands-On Help Line" is 01992 500 530.*
***Colin Rees***